# My Proper Life

## Poems 1975-2017

_John Richmond_ (signature)

## John Richmond

First published simultaneously in Australia and UK 2017

Chalkface Press P/L

Perth    London
Australia   &   England

chalkface@icloud.com
www.chalkface.net.au

National Library of Australia Cataloguing-in-Publication entry:

Creator:   Richmond, John, 1951- author.
Title:      My proper life : poems 1975 - 2017 / John Richmond.

ISBN:    9781875136360 (hardback)

Subjects:   Poetry--21st century.
           Autobiographical poetry, English.

Printed and bound in England by Short Run Press Ltd, Exeter, Devon

For Peter Hetherington

# Contents

## 2.

## 3.

## 4.

## 6.

# To the Reader

I hear you ask, 'Is this the lot
and such a long time passed?'
Disguise the glum fact I cannot:
the headcount isn't vast.

I hope you find some poems here,
though little and though late,
which light the mind or please the ear
and have been worth the wait.

You will, if in your thoughts one stays
after you turn its page,
redeem the outlay of my days
although I took an age.

# 1

# The Entertainer

Sometimes, after tea, when my brothers and I
played in the garden, I sensed at the window
our parents' faces, and knew that they were happy.

This made me want to orchestrate the play,
being the eldest, the impresario,
but still present a seeming spontaneity,

watchful in case the game flagged or a quarrel broke out.
It mattered somehow to put on a show
which proved we were that family I'd heard about:

where parents wash the tea things, talking quietly
and children play as they are meant to do –
under smiling eyes, under an elm tree.

# Elijah

*To my father at 60*

He sat down under a juniper tree
and wished that he might die.
*I am not better than my fathers*
was his complaint and cry.

The story always pleased me as a child.
The way it named the tree –
the particular kind he sat down under –
started my sympathy.

The phrase itself – *not better than my fathers* –
I never understood.
Admitting such a gauge of our condition
took me until manhood.

# Martha, Mary and Housework

*To my mother*

The only time you criticised the Word
was over that story. It was plain unjust that He
sent Martha away, while Mary sat dreaming and idling all day,
*taking that good part,* maybe.
You took Martha's part, without apology.

# Upturn

*To my father at 70*

The state wants to check that you're still safe to drive
so you're wise to take up gliding. Think of ageing
simply as travel with the extra dimension.

Pause long enough here at the biblical span
to upturn the hourglass, set the bonus years running.

Loop the loop. Think of the past
as the change from your pockets which falls to the grass
when you stand on your head in the park.

# Bicycles

*To my father at 80*

'A father's no shield
for his child.' Robert Lowell, 'Fall 1961'

It's spring of 1962, a Saturday,
I'm with my father on an empty-at-the-weekend train,
    and full of joy.
We're on our way to buy a bicycle, my first.

We come back on the same suburban train.
(I know; I checked the number; I am in that phase.)
The bike I chose is blue, and in the guard's van.
I suggest we get off one stop earlier than planned
so I can try it on the road.
My father is unsure, and then consents.

The hill from Beckenham to Shortlands,
in the valley of the Ravensbourne, is steep.
We're at the top. He holds the bike.
I mount, and wobble, then shoot off and leave him standing.

At the bottom, I turn round
and watch him running down the hill
and when he's close enough I see
fear clearing from his eyes.
But I'm all right

and 42 years pass

and we are in a shop in Bedford, buying him a bicycle.
He's 80, and the old one is beyond repair.
He mounts outside the shop,
adjusts the saddle height,
then says he'll ride the five miles home
and will I take the car? He'll see me there.

I follow at a distance, not to seem concerned.
I stop in driveways, watch him wobble on the new machine,
then overtake by half a mile, and stop and wait again. Each time
fear has its hand around my heart.
These roads which once were country now are chock-a-block
    with metal
and the bends are blind. Each time

he reappears. He is all right.

Great chapters of our lives have opened, closed.
A zero interim. Where but from the man ahead
have I inherited
this instinct of protectiveness for him?

# A Child's Farewell

*In memoriam Ivor John Richmond, died 6 April 2009*
*and Daphne Marion Richmond, died 6 May 2009*

## 1.

I told her he had died.
She said he'd gone ahead to his reward,
then calmly turned to telephoning, writing letters,
dealing with the surpluses of other people's grief.

Their separation was a little month
until I turned to telephoning, writing letters,
dealing with the surpluses of other people's grief.

To me, their sixty years' acquaintance was a long road, jointly
    travelled, at an end.
To them, it was the courting prelude to a marriage
where their spoiled and shrunken bodies would be beautiful again,
as in this photograph I keep deep in my wallet:

field, hedge, sunlight on branches, and the two of them;
he's laughing at the camera,
she's riding on his shoulders,
loose skirt sexily hoicked up behind his neck,
hands holding on to handfuls of his thick black hair,
for balance partly, mainly for desire.

## 2.

And yet I think there was a doubt in her.
He never doubted, never ceased to sing God's praises, utter in strange
    tongues,
convinced that when the light of this world failed
the moment's darkness would be but the blinking of his eyelids
to adjust to greater light.  His faith was bottomless.

Her illness broke her slowly, like a torturer.
*Please, Jesus, where is God in this?* she sometimes wondered.
*Should I call this 'testing'?  Just suppose*
*that all this time I've...*  She refused the thought.
But fear was in the bedroom where her children smiled at her.
'Open a window, please.'  The night air brought relief.

## 3.

'My body's fine; my mind is shot.'
The theologian/scientist/inventor
asks me how my work is going
how my work is going
how my work is going.
I reply in even tones each time.
I tell him, 'Dad, suppose you broke your leg
and afterwards you limped. You wish it hadn't happened
but it's not a cause for shame.'
He sees the logic, but it doesn't help.
My mother calls. Straightway he runs upstairs.
I hear their voices, not their words.
He runs downstairs again. 'Now what was it she wanted?'
I go up to check.

## 4.

Her mind is fine; her body's shot.
Head girl/head teacher holds the household reins
as firmly as she used to in her strength.
In bed, she plans the supermarket order (internet),
the pre-cooked frozen lunches order (telephone);
from dozens of mail-order catalogues
she chooses plants and thermal underwear and birthday gifts.
She keeps up correspondence (missionaries from Jordan to Nepal to
    hearten,
relative in Kent – bad-tempered all her life – to soothe,
and widows scattered over England to supply with news).

Most constant of her duties: give instructions to her constant
    husband
so the milk will not run short,
the teas-made will be filled,
the back doors will be double-locked at night.
He's tagged, when out of earshot, by the cordless phones they use as
    intercom.

I'm sitting with him down the garden on a bench beyond the fruit
    trees.
Coffee time. A blackbird speaking from the hedge.
He smiles and listens. 'Now we're out of range.'

## 5.

A misery they carried all their married days:
the self-inflicted murder of the happy brain
to set at nought the useful pleasures of this life
before the coming Judgment of the unredeemed.

This coloured all, spoiled all. No hope, achievement, love
could live outside that grand delusion feared as fact.
A stupid certainty! My father's journal:
*Daphne doesn't want to go to heaven*
*unless she knows that all her children will be there one day.*

Don't tell me, when we scattered ashes, his and hers,
handful after handful given to the air where peewits called
and sky and cliffs and sea observed but kept their distance;
don't you tell me, as the ashes touched the turf,
that somehow, then or at some day of reckoning,
my parents were or would be somewhere else.

### 6.

My father's epigram: 'The only thing
to do about your parents is forgive them.'
Here's a child, in homage to his father
stepping back along the separating path he took
to where their ways divided.
He pursues the single pathway further
till it opens on a park, an afternoon.
A man and boy are playing cricket. For the boy
the game is purest happiness, the surest proof of love.
Neither is aware of being watched. The only thing
the solitary spectator, standing there,
can do about the young man playing cricket with his son
is offer, not forgiveness, but his thanks.

# Over Tennyson Down

How strange that I, six times a year,
should now fly back and forth
over the place where mum and dad
went courting in their youth
and low enough to fix the spot
where they rejoined the earth.

How strange that they, for sixty years,
believed the simple lie
that death is but the passport to
reunion in the sky
and joyful recognition that
the righteous cannot die.

And were they face to face with God
while we, through darkened glass,
caught only glimpses of the truth
of what had come to pass
as, emptying their plastic urns,
we spilled them on the grass?

My dears, you thought the fable true:
your ashes re-collected,
your youthful beauty formed anew,
your bodies resurrected.
Alas! That I look down on you
is not what you expected.

# Evening Visitor

I met my father's ghost last night
as I was putting tools back in the garden shed.
He came up through the orchard, hopeful and recognising.
I was in my overalls and so was he.

I said, 'Dad, what are you doing here?
I thought you didn't like France:
food too rich, wrong kind of Christianity.
The day we tipped your ashes on the Isle of Wight
I thought that's where you'd stay.'

He said, 'My boy, I've come to tell you
that I was mainly wrong and you were mainly right,
but only mainly. There *is* a heaven;
it's like an autumn morning
when the gentle sun is warm on the face
but there's a fresh wind too and leaves are twisting in the air
and both kinds of chestnut fall with the stronger gusts,
thumping the grass.'

                    'What do you do all day?'

'We walk about. Sometimes we exchange a word.
Mostly we just smile and wave at a distance,
knowing how agreeable everything is.
John, I'm sorry that I spent so much of my life in fear
when there was nothing to be afraid of.
And because you loved me and I was your dad
I made you fearful too. Now I discover
that there's all sorts over there:

---

Roman Catholics, Muslims, Jews... every religion,
plus people like you, seekers after truth
not expecting a second innings
and pleasantly surprised to get one.

I want to confess something.
I married your mother so I could have sex without shame
and the price was: belief.
Then the children came, and she and I were happy for a while,
and we were sure we'd found the only truth.
But you grew up and left us, and we couldn't understand
how most of you could be so casual
about your everlasting souls.

I wish I'd known.'

I said, 'Dad, I grew up a long time ago.
I stopped being afraid when I was twelve.
I remember the occasion. We were in church, the vicar going on as
     usual,
and suddenly, like a gift, I knew that he and mum and you and I
were tiny, in space and time. That what I was hearing was one voice
and that the world contained a million voices, and always had.
I saw the universe turned inside out.
What I'd thought was everything was only... a thing.
Of course, I didn't own up to such a revelation at the time.
It would have caused unpleasantness. But later
I couldn't help it when the great gulf opened out between us.
I told myself it was your problem, not mine.

And I remember another day, when I was 25,
when I kissed you. Not just hugged you in a manly sort of way;
I kissed you. You jumped back about three feet
but you were glad. And after that we always kissed,
like Italian men, and we were easy.

I have to thank you for loving poetry
and for having books of poetry at home for me to wander in,
when you weren't literary. Why shouldn't a physicist
quote Matthew Arnold by the yard?
And remember when I took you into hospital
not long before the end? You had two books:
the Bible and the *Rubaiyat of Omar Khayyam*.
I said it looked to me as if you were hedging your bets.
We read the whole of the *Rubaiyat* aloud to each other in the ward.
I don't suppose St George's Tooting had ever heard anything like it.

And I've already written (but I'll say it again)
about the hours and hours you gave me, playing cricket
when I was a boy. They secured our love,
which no amount of strife over religion could dislodge.
I loved you, dad, and because I loved you and you knew it
I haven't been regretful since you've gone,
but I just miss you. There.
Why are you wearing overalls? Do you get issued with them?'

'No,' he said, 'I wondered if you needed a hand.
You always used to help me when you were at home.'

I said, 'You're a bit late. I've more or less finished for today,
but thanks anyway. I'll be in the garden
these next few afternoons if the weather holds.
Come and see me when you're free.' He smiled and nodded,
hesitated, as if he still had more to say,
as if our talk had partly, not completely, satisfied
the longing in him; then he went his way
down through the wood just as the sun
had touched the treetops on the valley's other side.

# Thinking about Heaven

I lay, and thought about heaven.
I was eight. The ceiling offered no clue.
The problem was not: *Am I going?*
but: *When I get there, what do I do?*

The show, they said, would run and run
forever. That was my major fear.
However pleasant what you did there was,
how would it feel in its millionth year?

I sensed a nightmare coming on.
The principal task was to comprehend
how big heaven is in time and space;
to size it up from end to end.

I panicked when I saw an endless line
of rods of time laid whitely in the gloom
forever and forever; would not say amen
to that infinite horror in the room.

The curtains flickered in the night.
Groaning, I prayed for sleep, which came.
Afterwards, they told me that *eternal*
and *everlasting* are not the same,

that heaven is eternal, outside time,
which measurement of years or miles cannot record.
Later, I had my appendix out
and got a notion of the great reward

as a sort of anaesthetic
and Jesus as the surgeon with the knife.
This model served a stopgap purpose
until the time came in my life

when the problem didn't figure any more.
Heaven has receded, but earth designs
equivalent dilemmas, and the ceiling still
encodes its messages in cracks and lines.

# Non Credo

I have said no, on the evidence, and mainly in my strength
face cheerfully the entail.
Besides, it is a worn-out argument to most, not worth
the brain's energy and the while.
We are material.
The world of matter urgently requires us here.
God is not, and his dad
was not a carpenter.

I am conscious; consciousness is better than oblivion.
Yet I consent to be nothing
when the time comes; or if, against the odds, there is some transposition,
for that too I am willing.
At least one thing is certain:
no grand examiner will name the good and evil.
Heaven and hell are not.
Hereafter is a level.

Yes, put it down like that. When some mornings bring a loss of nerve,
when suddenly I am surprised by fear,
when the circus of texts and images sees its chance to revive,
that will do for an answer.
We are responsible.
Our actions and our loves will be the verdict on our stay.
If not we, then no one
makes a difference either way.

# Eclipses

'"Then shall the sun be turned to darkness and the moon to blood…"'
I know about eclipses from an elder of the church.
He says we should expect the Lord to give these portents now.
God's people, as in Joel's day, must daily wait and watch.

I'm in the audience at Stratford. It's my first *King Lear*.
Myopic, superstitious Gloucester, troubled at the sight:
'These late eclipses of the sun and moon portend no good
to us…' I think: about astrology, Edmund was right.

This cloudless, freezing night in March, I'm gazing at the sky
– at far-flung, automatic bodies falling into line;
the earth, the sun's dumb slave, in silent mastery of its moon –
and wondering at the workings of the heavenly machine.

I'm not the first, nor best, to press his wonder into verse.
I'm reading disbelieving Hardy, following his thought
that in a motion so ordained and calm, 'so small a shade',
can be confined the beauty and confusion we have wrought.

# Birthplace

October sunshine, high on the down,
a view of the city, the harbour, the sea:
the place where I started I cannot disown;
its marks are indelibly printed on me,
grown into my flesh as their bearer has grown
like flukes in the bark of this sycamore tree.

Whatever the healing that knowledge has brought
in banishing nightmares of childish belief;
in spite of my credo of rational thought –
'Inhabit the days, for the daylight is brief' –
the marks on my mind from the pox that I caught
are like spots on the skin of this sycamore leaf.

## Christmas Atheist

The holly from my trees within.
The wood smoke from my fire without.
I leave the house and walk my ground
to take December's failing pulse.

Quite still.  Quite silent.  Buzzard.  Wren.
This festive walker's glad at heart
to know with undeluded mind:
there's human love, and nothing else.

# Crisis? What Crisis?

The world had held its breath, supposedly.
Throughout my teens, when others reminisced
about the week they thought the world might end,
I kept a puzzled quiet, wondering
where I had been when some had prayed aloud
and some had taken final walks in parks;
too proud to show my ignorance
by asking them what was this unity in fear
which I had been excluded from.

One night at university I tracked back
after such a conversation
and came to my appendix operation.

The pain that day; too ill to go to school;
the doctor's diagnosis and his phone call to the ambulance;
the hospital; the surgeon telling me to count to ten
(I got to three); the ward where I woke up;
and then a week's – that week's – recuperation.

Russian ships steamed south towards the waiting silos.
Kennedy sat with his generals. I lay in bed
without a radio, and read of war in Germany or space
in *Biggles* and *The Eagle*. For relief
I laughed at *Jennings* till the stitches hurt.
The vicar visited. My father came each night,
afraid for all of us, but saying nothing of it.

By the time the vicar drove me home,
the ships were steaming north, the crisis past.
The conversations I rejoined
had right-about-turned to the usual.
The world had breathed again, supposedly.

If memory were physical, I'd say
it doesn't hurt to touch that place in me
which stirs an ache in others, when I see
myself tucked up in bed with books to read,
the innocent
as Armageddon came and went.

# Learning to Whistle

Walking in the park, I came up behind a boy
– of nine or ten – learning to whistle.
A tuneless tangle of notes
and breath where notes should have been.
I slowed my pace, and followed him,
since I was suddenly that boy
– of nine or ten – learning to whistle.
Such patience! And the need to be alone.
What is it in the brain
that teaches tongue and lips
the small adjustments
– infinitely small and deftly quick –
that turn a tube of air to music?
Beethoven's Fifth, the *Marseillaise*,
the theme tune to *The Archers*:
I can do them all!
A talent once learned, never lost,
and disregarded till the boy I once was
is there ahead of me,
rehearsing alone in the park.

# Near Tralee: July 1970

'Now you look like an educated man,' the woman says.
'What's that thing mean? I got it for a present from my sons.
From France.'

I read the motto on the little plate hung on the wall
of this, the first non-risky bedroom Angela and I have shared
since we embarked on this, the first discovery of fleshly joy
of both our lives, and rediscovered, scarcely credited, each night
in this, the house the woman owns.

In golden letters:
*Faire l'amour avec une femme sans ôter sa chemise*
*C'est manger un orange sans l'éplucher.*

'It means,' I say,
'To love a woman is a joy as sweet
As eating oranges in sunshine.'

'Well that's nice,' the woman says, and looks at each of us.
I look at Angela. She's looking out the window,
fighting back mirth, and fiddling with the ring she went and bought.

The woman adds, with emphasis, 'I wish you both that joy yourselves,
and when the children come.' Outfacing my straight face.

# Self-portrait

The truth is that I like the face I've got, the way it is.
I like the days when mirrors meet me often; take each chance
to check that I can say, again, 'Not bad for 52,
for 53… You're looking good since half an hour ago.
The skin below the eyes does sag a bit, it's true, and yes,
there is some looseness at the neck. So what?'

Cosmetic surgeons' bright insinuating knives will not
come near the baggy, lumpy, veiny bits my DNA
has programmed for me, readying to bud, to bloom each year
I've yet to greet. I won't let Botox grip my features in
a rictus of surprise the more incongruous now that
I find I raise my eyebrows less and less.

And Clarins, Clinique, Garnier, ingenious mountebanks
who sigh to women that their youth's a stuff will not endure
unless they try this stuff of seaweed, cucumber or birch,
extracted, potted, packaged, branded, sold: don't ever think
about a range of extra-firming facial masks for me.
(You have? Do me a favour. Save your breath.)

No instrument, no poison, nor no cream will tuck or smooth
this riddling record of my life away; make disappear
its evidence of actions, passions, thoughts, conceived and done
in public, private, secret; wipe the marks of love and lust,
of laughter, anger, concentration, joy in beauty from
the portrait of the accident I am.

Four postcard portraits gaze across my desk: four great old men,
all heroes of the wooden O, the stage, renowned throughout
the little O, the earth. Why should this minor talent seek
to change his even littler O, his face, when Jonson's warts
and Beckett's corrugations, Gielgud's, Miller's hairless domes
are promises of beauty yet to come?

My face I wash with soap to keep it clean. Life does the rest.
One derogation from this strict regime I must admit.
My lover hates the hairs which now accelerate from both
my nostrils. I can see her point. We don't know where they've been.
She clips them for me. They're the only sign of facial age
the world (except for her) has never seen.

# On His Circumcision

Grazing on-line, I came across a group of males last night,
all Christians, all Americans, determined to put right
a wrong done to their manhood which they saw as child abuse:
entire they had been born, and yet they wanted a prepuce.

This gross intrusion on their persons their attorneys meant
to challenge in the courts and thus to set a precedent
that no one – even those by holy laws and customs bound –
should be obliged to suffer this humiliating wound.

Their forum offers consolation, counsel, and advice
to those prepared to pay a multi-thousand-dollar price
to plastic surgeons, all acknowledged masters of their art,
who would by artificial means re-graft the tender part
onto the stump of flesh from which it was untimely torn.

(And should this seem, they say, a costly sacrifice to make,
what matters comfort or expense, when principle's at stake?)

I'm neither Jew nor Muslim but, when I was hardly born,
somebody took a knife to me in 1951,
and am I, as this website says, thereby deprived of fun?
How should I know?  It may be that a dulling of sensation
enhances carnal pleasure through delayed ejaculation.
I won't add *my* name to the list of those who would accuse
the perpetrators of a cut they could not then refuse.
In fact I'm glad I was a neonate when I was nipped,
unlike poor Tristram Shandy, pissing when a window slipped.

The world is woeful. There are battles worthier to win
than one whose cause is but the loss of half an inch of skin.
Marked men we are, but I don't feel resentful on that score.
If I were boastful (but I'm not) I might say, 'Less is more.'

## Internal Eclogue at 60

'The wind in the oaks is a creature of springtime,
a shaper of clouds as they fly.
The last of the frosts has kept clear of the blossom
and primroses pattern the wall.
Soon the corn will change colour, the summer will open,
and swifts will scream at the sky:
*The living know that they have to die*
*and the dead know nothing at all.*

The wind in the oaks is a creature of autumn.
The firewood is stacked in the dry.
The weight of my apples has broken some branches –
the excess can rot where they fall.
A child who is 60, who questions the Preacher,
is armoured against the reply:
*The living know that they have to die*
*and the dead know nothing at all.*'

\*

'Excuse me if I interrupt this melancholy strain;
I feel an urge to bluntly re-acquaint you with the truth.
(You've had this weakness for Ecclesiastes since your youth.)
You've lived among the lucky. You've no business to complain.

Welfare state boy: who can tell? You could have 30 years to run.
You're healthy, handsome, solvent. Greatest gift of all: you're loved.
Had pagan gods existed, they'd have seen you and approved.
*Quos dei amant iuvenes moriuntur* – not in your case, son.

So take my tip: shake off those Bible blues – *All flesh is grass* –
and go and mow the lawn – Voltaire's correct philosophy.
Despite – or should I say because of – our mortality,
I see it didn't take you long to get your Freedom Pass!'

## 'The Leaving It'

When my time comes to 'shuffle off', to sling my hook,
to pop my clogs, to contemplate the river's brink,
to settle my account and close the book,
to make my way through emigration
to 'the undiscover'd country' where – it would be nice to think –
they have a well stocked library-cum-lounge-bar in the sky

will I

find consolation as I go 'into that good night', good day,
with friends around the bed, drinking champagne,
they out of glasses, I – once more a baby – from a beaker with a straw,
light-headed but still functioning,
the pain kept chemically at bay;

or

with a stream of filthy curses,
final flailings of a drug-befuddled brain
staring at doom,
betray its secrets better hid,
the lid embarrassingly lifted on the id,
causing firm and kindly nurses
rapidly to wheel me to a private room?

The manner of too many deaths I've seen suggests
I may be forced to make my last requests
by merest movements: twitchings of an eyebrow,
liftings of one trembling finger somehow signalling assent, dissent.
The watchers over me will ask each other what I meant.

To very few is granted
an exit all of us have thought about and wanted:
the gentlest change of element, of gear,
a ceasing of the heartbeat in mid-sleep,
departure unaware,
the parachutist taking to the steady air,
the swimmer welcomed to the deep, without indignity or fear.

The Plymouth Brethren taught me as a boy
to hope that we, the righteous,
would escape death's agony and Tribulation's woe
completely; we'd be 'taken' in the Rapture, captured,
caught up, levitated, holy parachutists in reverse,
to meet our Saviour in the atmosphere
(joy unconfined, though altitude unspecified)
and join the resurrected saints who had already died.
And this might happen any time: next week, next year,
tomorrow… What a way to go!
Despite my early tendency to vertigo,
each night I would rehearse the prayer
that I might be included in that hovering in air…

Useless. God wasn't listening. I knew His wrath
was terrible; to me, it seemed, His ear was cloth.

Well, that's all finished with. It's hard now to believe
that I believed it then. I won't be up there in the ranks,
panoptic, recognising, 'face to face'. Earthly metaphors
will do for me: clogs, hooks. So when they call my number
(not the roll that's called up yonder)
for what I'll have received (I say my grace)
I hope I'll have enough puff to give thanks.

# Prayer before Death

*After Louis MacNeice*

I'm due to depart: so hear me.
My funeral ship on the slipway is set
  and I shall be carried
    wherever the winds and the tides of unknowing will steer me.

I'm due to depart: surround me.
I have need of the presence of friends
  lest the nearness of death and the breath of its mouth
    on my forehead confound me.

I'm due to depart: behind me
are the years I inhabited joyfully, I
  who might never have happened at all,
    but I happened, I was, I was glad
      of the gift of the years, O remind me.

I'm due to depart: please read me
lines from the poets I loved, who could
  sing in a fashion which brought me to tears,
    who got to the point of the thing,
      who would always, I knew and accepted, exceed me.

I'm due to depart: forgive me –
some token I want that my work was not wasted,
  that words I have spoken or written have lasted,
    that actions I've taken for good will outlive me.

I'm due to depart: believe me
when I say that my heartbeat, though faltering now,
   till nearly this moment has quickened with anger
      when greed and stupidity, cruelty, violence swaggered unchallenged.
         That girl on the ground in her blood will not leave me.

I'm due to depart: replay me
one moonrise at midnight, one mew of a buzzard who circles at noon,
   one start of a hare in the wood. All that beauty!
      The places we visited, times we have had:
         one evening, with laughter and wine, is enough.
            The goodness of friendship, the greatness of love:
               life promised me plenty, and didn't betray me.

Don't foolishly tell me that out there you'll meet me.
Launch me and my ship down the slipway. Complete me.

# 2

---

To Helen Savva

# Hôtel des Medicis

We learn within chance walls to speak
the language of desire. We think ourselves unique.
This sweet code, practised *sotto voce*, translates ill.
Outside, the only clues we offer are oblique:
your way of sitting in a café chair, my smile.
The public has no inkling of our skill.

## Bons Appétits 1977

A simple formula:
wake up, make love,
ignore the maid who's knocking at the door
who says she's cleaned all other rooms, below, above
and cannot wait for us a moment more.

Some time later
stroll out to breakfast in the brown café.
Big coffees, bread and jam and *pains au chocolat*
will set us up to walk
(the only way to travel)
all over Paris, randomly, all day,
stopping to watch
in every park, on any piece of gravel,
the *parties de pétanque* at play.

Back in the hotel at six
make love, and shower.
Then, freshly dressed,
step forth into the hour of the *apéritif*
on the pavement outside the green bar.
The air is still
the evening luminous with limes in leaf
and we could eat a horse. We will.

Squeezed onto benches, no elbow room to spare,
we dine where once dined Valéry and Gide.
No literary pleasure can exceed
the joy of *filets de hareng, steaks chevalins* and *frites,*
*roquefort,* apple tarts,

at least two litres of *vin ordinaire.*
The toilet is listed at the Ministry of Arts.

On to the red bar for several *digestifs.*
Back to the hotel at two.
No stars, no lift. Creep up ten flights.
Make love, approximately, and sleep,
omitting to turn off the lights.

Repeat this for eleven days and nights.

Such steady pleasures. And such appetites.

## Topless is More

How well equipped you look!
You've left behind the working year,
its cumbersome cargo.
Just one or two items of mandatory gear:
bikini bottoms, and a book
published by Virago.

# Your Morning Yoga

I like to watch you, naked, out of bed
and pointing skyward. You salute the sun
with curtains closed and bedside lamp switched on.

I'm happy that you use the bathroom first.
It gives me precious extra time alone
to play the foetus and deny the man.

I do this every day. So why, today,
has childish grief invaded my routine
with sudden, useless tears I can't contain

for thinking of a time, I pray to God
to make it distant, let it not be soon,
when I won't see you in that pose again?

## Strawberries

Feed me strawberries in my mouth
this afternoon of youth.
The sun is hot, the road is clear
and we are heading south.

Feed me strawberries in my mouth:
food of a long romance.
The corn is ageing in the fields
this harvest time in France.

Feed me strawberries in my mouth.
Agree not to arrive.
I'll suck them off your fingers' ends
as long as I can drive.

## Sunday Morning

In the simple morning light
I feel your breathing on my arm.
Breath of laughter, voice of charm:
I'm in no hurry. I expect
your waking kiss,

claiming many mornings more,
awake in bed, not saying much,
relying on desire of touch;
as many yet, I wish, as from
our first, to this.

# Anniversary

The lovely woman with the cold vermouth
is waiting for me halfway up the stairs.
I'm still distracted by her laughing mouth
this end-of-summer evening, 30 years
since first she waited where she said she would
and walked beside me to the river's edge.
We spoke some words which linked our lives for good:
an awkward but sufficient lovers' pledge.

Tonight, the sullen skies unload their rain.
I turn the lights on and pick out some jazz:
Ben Webster, *Stormy Weather.* Time to dine,
or not. The ice cubes in her tumbler shine,
she makes her eyes round in that way she has,
I follow her. Ben plays that strain again.

# Confession

When first I said I loved you, I confess I was afraid
of what those words had signed me up to; had I just made
an inadvertent contract which could never be unsigned?

And later, when the statement was a habit of our speech,
I still kept an escape clause, for my comfort, out of your reach
in a locked drawer of the cabinet of my secret mind.

It stayed there for years, as insurance, a hedge for my bet,
as if, after the swoon of our life together, I might yet
fall to earth with a bump, and rub my eyes, and need to get out.

In *your* mind, from the start, our claim on each other was free.
You had no foolish phobia about being stuck with me
and with the unlooked-for luggage which love brings; no nagging
    doubt.

What was I so afraid of all those thousands of spendthrift days
when people had long ago joined our names up in a phrase
and we smiled for the camera, an item, a couple, a pair?

Did I seriously imagine some truer life elsewhere?

I don't recall.
There is no paper in the drawer.
There is no truer life I'm looking for.
Before it gets too late, my darling,
may I again just state
how much, imperfectly, I love you, luggage and all?

# Rendezvous

When, after this long time together, I'm standing waiting for you
    in a square,
and knowing you'll contrive to turn up late,
preferring me to be there first, preferring not to wait alone
and I not minding, I quite liking letting slip
these minutes of my life, now here, now gone,
because, I hope, I have so much of it to spare:
the waiting brings a quickening of heartbeat
for the moment when we'll meet as in the early days,
when I would fix my gaze upon you, coming through the crowd,
an almost stranger in a public place,
looking about you, searching for me; then your recognising face.

# CDs

Pick out Debussy this evening;
do it for me.
Watch with me, love, as the sunset
torches the sea.
Sometimes I get sentimental,
weighing the years.
Pour us a drink as the nocturnes
bring me to tears.

Bring on Ravel, now the moonlight
bleaches the sand:
music to waltz to – so shall we?
Give me your hand.
No one will play for us later;
later is soon.
One two three, heavily, lightly,
under the moon.

# The Stalker

An angled rain goes darting
into our tousled lawn.
The six-week drought is over.

The hare who crops the grasses
is questioning the air,
his ears erect for danger.

My slow steps down the garden
at length disturb the hare.
He looks, and does not linger.

The hour-long downpour passes.
Shadows are reborn.
The sun brings forth a reader.

The reader is my lover.
She lounges in a chair,
her feet up on another,

as when our love was starting.
Thank God she didn't scare
when first I went towards her.

# One in a Bed

'A marriage is that state where man and wife
are each prepared to swear the other party snores.'
My love, this is no legal separation, not a cause
for weeping and for lamentation if your breath of life
drives me to seek the blessed silence of a distant room.
Pay no attention to Ecclesiastes; in our case
desire not fails, it's simply put on hold; that's no disgrace.
We know what Marvell says: there's no embracing in a tomb,
and so goodnight; our parting's *au revoir* and not adieu.
When morning comes, I'm coming back to you.

## Three in a Bed

Last night I came to bed and found, to my great pain,
another with you in our sheets. I am to blame;
night after night I've sat up reading while you've lain
and lonely shivered. Want of comfort overcame
at last your long, too much assumed, fidelity.
I've had my head in Homer. You, Penelope,
having rebuffed all rival suits, have had resort
to this... this... I must call it... thing. And I had thought
that I was all you needed as a source of heat.
I was your male equivalent of Abishag.
Age is upon us when, to warm you, I compete
with water boiled and bulging in a rubber bag.

# Shadows are Ageless

Shadows are ageless. These that we throw
this evening on our walk are those we threw
when first we walked – 'walked out' – together. Now, as then,
the setting sun exaggerates our differences
but silhouettes forgive, ignore the work of time.
And they do well, in that, whatever mirrors,
disappointing flatterers, may say,
this simple light effect maintains the greater truth:
black on a ground of gold, as constant as our hearts.

# Laughing over Books

She's up there in the bedroom, reading in bed.
She likes the horizontal; she's enclosed.
He's down here by the fireside in his usual chair.
He shuns the horizontal; needs an upright back.
Adjacent, both are far away in books
as evening tends to night, the day becomes the morrow.
Rarely, in the silence, upward or downward,
the one sends laughter softly to the other,
and each is grateful for the unintended gift,
the overflow of pleasure from the reader's mind.

# Tracks

An out-of-season Monday, and the beach
as far as we can see is ours alone.
October sunshine burnishes the waves;
the wind flicks up their fringes as they break.
We're at a time of life which comprehends
that days like this are precious things to hold
and not to use as inexhaustible.
The tracks we made when walking up the beach
it pleases us to notice, walking back.
The tide is rising. Briefly, they were us:
apart, together. Never out of touch.

# Our Time

There was a time when I was not.
A time will come when I won't be.
Between these aeons, there's a dot,
a microscopic speck. That's me.

What biochemical event
how many billion years ago
began the process that has meant
that when I say, 'I love you so,'

those vowels and consonants affect
the air, your eardrums and your brain
in ways the higher intellect
cannot sufficiently explain?

The heart's a bit of pumping gear.
It's prone to blockages and leaks.
Some other force must engineer
that flush of colour in your cheeks:

some impulse, some primaeval need,
before we learned to stand up straight,
implanted in the human breed
so I don't have too long to wait

for your familiar reply,
'I love you too. I love you more,'
which grants me courage to defy
the dark behind, the dark before.

# 3

# The Fall from National Esteem of a Poet Laureate

Not long before he died, Sir John
on prime-time television spoke
a word not in the lexicon
of nicely brought-up English folk.

The viewers were appalled. They knew
that other poets curse and swear
– a godless, socialistic crew –
but not the nation's teddy bear.

And later in the series, he
made matters worse when he averred
he had not done sufficiently
the act to which the word referred.

Unhappy is the laureate's lot!
His function is to celebrate
the deed by which we're all begot
but as performed by heads of state:

I mean, commemorate in rhyme
its prelude at the altar stair;
then, after an appropriate time,
its outcome as a sceptre's heir.

Worse were Sir John's official toils;
his by-appointment pen was forced
to brown-nose various junior royals
who married, reproduced, divorced.

Amid this rife fecundity
it's not surprising he was vexed;
his life, he told us on TV,
had under-served the over-sexed.

Too late to remedy the lack.
A dead-end job, a paltry wage
(a hundred pounds, a butt of sack):
the f-word was a cry of rage,

however ruefully expressed,
of one who knew the days were gone
when he might hope to be undressed
by tennis girls who turned him on.

# A Song for England

*To Stephen Eyers*

*The Rev. Donald Allister of Cheadle refused the request of Victoria Williams and her fiancé that the hymn 'Jerusalem' be sung at their wedding. His defence of the decision was that the words of the hymn were too nationalistic. (He also forbad 'I Vow to Thee My Country', for the same reason.) On 11 August 2001, the letters page of* The Daily Telegraph *contained nine letters debating Mr Allister's action.*


'Absolutely right decision,' writes the Reverend Andrew Price.
'Christian principles of marriage; sober, dignified advice
to be found in Cranmer's Prayer Book, that's what these young
        people need;
not the musings of a mystic without benefit of creed.'


Mr Morley's language makes the views of Mr Price look wet.
Blake for him's as dangerous as 'deranged heretics' can get.
'Theologically, "Jerusalem" is nonsense, total rot.'
*And did those feet...?* The answer's clear to Morley. 'They did not.'


Mr Lennox thinks it helpful to insult the virgin pair.
'Quite unsuitable for marriage, in a church or anywhere.'
Why does Lennox push them down the path of immorality?
'People like them only know the hymns they pick up on TV.'

Feeling better, gentlemen, delivered of such fine tirades?
Listen to a soft reply from this side of the barricades.
Fellow Englishmen, for love of England, where we all belong,
some of us would like that poem to become our nation's song.

We think it would do much better, as a national cement,
than the set of crude commands, prosodically incompetent,
sending God about his business, Union Jack stamped on his brow
(written for a German monarch), which we have to stomach now.

★

I should like to wish the couple in their early married life
all the happiness we know that William Blake had with his wife.
Grains of sand contain whole worlds for those with inner eyes to
    look.
Liberated souls can have the joy of sex without a book.

★

This year Christ came, incognito, stepping onto Cornwall's shore
as the legend says he might have done two thousand years before.
Much had altered, so he noted, as he moved around the land:
not ungreen, and not unpleasant. Twenty centuries he scanned

sitting in a pub one evening, with the papers and a beer.
Ireland, Palestine… and then he saw the letters quoted here.
Echo of raised voices, was it, faint across the interim,
sneering, knowing, briefly caused the countenance divine to dim?

# The Walker

Already old when pointed out to me,
he was a special feature of the town:
the grocer's man (retired).  For forty years,
six days a week, he'd walked round villages
and farms, and stood at doors to write down lists
of groceries, the orders for the week:
a woman's voice, his fountain pen, his book.

This way of getting trade had had its day.
The grocer kept him on to 65,
then told him, kindly, that he'd have to stop.

No longer fit for work, but fit to walk,
at first the pensioner maintained the same
six routes, the same six days, for exercise;
he liked to be outside and on the go.
When modern traffic finally destroyed
his pleasure and his peace, he reckoned up
how many circuits of the small town park
would be an equal distance.  There he was:
black-suited, bowler-hatted, keeping count;
an object of amusement to the young.
To those who taunted him, he gave no sign.
To those who greeted him, he raised his hat.

He got to 93 before he died
one morning, pulling on his walking boots.
He'd done some mileage.  If he'd been a van
(that ancient first one that my father owned),
his clock would long ago have clicked beyond
the line of nines, then zeroes, back to one.

# Jewish Funeral

*In memoriam Rachael Farrar, teacher*

The wide field north of London slopes to woodland.
The little digger waits, its job half done.
The tolling voice, in English and in Hebrew,
consoles the living: life and death are one.

The sentences and prayers, like these gulls inland,
are tousled in the wind and flung away.
She said she knew her spirit wouldn't travel:
'The afterlife's a comfort and a lie.'

Her teacher's talent was to spot in learners
the impulse of a nameable idea.
She helped them name it, and the knowledge given
was something she denied had come from her.

The coffin settles by its chance companions.
The clay is rattling on the wood too soon.
The London children who have cause to thank her
are walking in their thousands round the town.

# After a Quarrel

She sat on a bench in the freezing night, in the rain.
He stood a hundred yards away, and watched her back.
They had cursed, driven the last oaths in the language
into one another's brain.
Now one dilemma faced them both:
how to step across the concrete, forgive, be forgiven,
get in the warm again, but not do it first.

# Bequest

*In memoriam Frederick Seymour, 1895–1981*

No conversation needed or desired.
I'm in the ward each evening, just to sit.
His occupation is to breathe, and mine
to listen for his voice inside my head.

The voice remembered likes to stick to facts.
He made a choice quite easily one day:
*I went down to the office to recruit.*
*Mornington Crescent. Then I went straight back*

*and told my mother that I'd volunteered.*
*She was upset. But I was right to go.*
*If I had waited till they called me up*
*I never would have lasted like I did.*

On Vimy Ridge, the doctor's orderly,
he sewed them into blankets, corpse by corpse.
*We took their boots off, and their ID chains,*
*that's all. I saw their faces. Bits of boys.*

The voice resists grandiloquence. It speaks
of perks and pains: *I got the better food*
*'cause I was looking after officers.*
*The tin hats made my hair fall out in weeks.*

He lasted till a shell undid his leg.
*The wound was bad enough to bring me home.*
*They drained the pus for ages, bowls of it*
from where the shrapnel nestled in the thigh

and lodges there tonight; a flake of iron
which cooled first in a factory in the Ruhr
now shivers with the rest of him inside
the shiny silver bag he's swaddled in.

Not long ago, at home, he handed me
a standard issue army greetings card,
address and message legible but faint,
the Allied flags still bright in coloured inks.

*My darling Dolly, my first chance to write.*
*Arrived quite safe in France on Monday last.*
*Am hoping you are well. Yours ever, Fred.*
*Goodbye dear* – like an afterthought, beneath.

The censor had approved these sentiments
and left his purple mark accordingly
but insufficient postage had been paid
by sender, and the message was delayed.

*Poor thing, she had to wait three months for this.*
*I kept it when she died. Look after it.*

No conversation needed or desired.
I'm in the ward each evening, just to sit.

# Thames between Greenwich and the Tower

Gun-metal grey, the river fills its channel
all the afternoon.  It hasn't finished yet.
It climbs the mosses on the warehouse walls.
Each flight of river stairs is drowned.

The southward swerve, the confidence,
the creature's own instinctive grace.

I've seen it in all lights today.
Today is March, and every season's miniature
has trafficked and paraded in the sky.
We've been through murk, hail, pelting winds
and suddenly a summer evening, so it seems,
where steady light stands blandly on the buildings.

At noon, two stumps of rainbow came and went,
set in a frame the slack commercial water,
bits of a geometric whole
whose bridging section was invisible.

Before the docks were built, uncorseted
the river would in season flood
the easy margins of its marsh.
They wharfed it in, made it work.

Three noisy centuries ran by.  Now every reach is idle.
Ratcliffe and Rotherhithe, Surrey Docks, London Docks: idle.
Three centuries crowned a few with wealth
argosied here from all the earth;
millions whose names have been forgotten
lived their side of that hard bargain.

Bypassed and unprofitable, the river's feathers ruffle,
change from grey to blue. The level tide slides seaward.
The day has turned its coat the final time
(I think) and left the bright side out.

## Pretty Polly Put the Kettle On

Take me home with you, please, Pretty Polly!
Our courtship has lasted too long.
I know you so well from a distance
that my hopes of a meeting are strong.

I spy you at Underground stations
while waiting for trains to come in;
you're wearing the sheerest of nylon
on your salmon-pink acres of skin.

You're immaculate here at Embankment
on the safe other side of the track.
No man will cross over to touch you
till the lucky bill-sticker comes back.

I think I can read the intention
behind these displays of your charms.
No matter which station I'm watching you at
you're inviting me into your arms.

*No I'm not! I'm the composite fancy*
*of some men in a marketing team.*
*They sat round a table and made me;*
*their image, their product, your dream.*

*And I have one distinct disadvantage*
*at the end of the length of your stare:*
*this form is a giant illusion;*
*I'm not, in reality, there.*

But I'm still coming home with you, Polly!
I'm too much in love to desist.
Oh please ask me up for a coffee;
let me show you you really exist.

I could help you take off all that nylon
far away from the Bakerloo Line.
I'd be yours, unvoyeuristically, Polly, I would
and you'd be, unsynthetically, mine.

# Express Dairy

I walked home from the station, silent street, sweating night.
A milk float hummed towards me, doing 40, quite a sight.

The milkman wore his firm's peaked cap, his own bare chest.
The woman sat beside him, blouse open, baby at breast.

They passed, and their mixed laughter echoed along the street.
There was no milk on the back, not at this hour, in this heat.

# Smokers at Greater London House, Camden Town

The cheerful addicts gather in a ring, pass packets round, share lights.
They stand beneath the beauteous façade of Greater London House:
Egyptian/deco/polychrome, restored. The offices within
are smoke-free zones. The comrades represent a perfect irony,
in self-inflicted exile from the same – then unpartitioned – space
where formerly Carreras manufactured Black Cat cigarettes
in quantities sufficient to reduce Britannia's breath to gasps.

A pair of black cat-statues, one on each side of the central doors,
completes the group; brand icons once, recast and reinstated now
as cats for cats' sake, emblems of pure style; immune to irony,
immune to sympathy for those to whom the Black Cat brought no
    luck...

Pyjama'd, wheezing, leaning on the sink, he coughs his morning
    phlegm.
They took away one lung, so walking's painful – she must have a
    smoke.
Drowning in air, he needs the oxygen – they fit the mask – too late.

The information of more recent years seems not to worry these,
our happy, kamikaze few, who hug their bodies, underdressed
for wet December twilight, toe their stubs out and go in again.

The cats are sleek with raindrops. Commerce? Art? It's all the same
    to them.

# Snowdrops

The northern year has rounded its dark cape
and pays out light in bonuses too mean for human eyes to note.
The sun has not been seen for days,
which pass us by without a recognising glance:
identical, anonymous.
There is no hope this side of Candlemas

except that snowdrops in the park are facts which work in these
     conditions.
It's a month since they received earth's first, faint, unmistakable
     instruction:
show themselves, resign themselves to soak, to freeze,
to sleep in snow, to break their necks on air, face ruin
weeks before the distant, gaudy date of spring's inauguration.

Here are the results, and here, and here again:
the new year's first accomplishment,
heads grouped and bowed and (not that it was asked for)
nodding their assent.

# Sunny Morning in the Park

A Christian men's group sits cross-legged on the grass.
They pray for guidance in their study of God's word.
Two groups of alcoholic men have made a start
on lager (extra strength), got from the Turkish shop.
The roses that my taxes pay for line the path
where laden shoppers, light of step, greet me with nods.
The child who rides the roundabout appeals in vain
for admiration from his parent, on the phone.
*Sweet day, so cool, so calm, so bright...* a luminance
inhabits these. The ordinary transfigured, blessed.

# Up All Night

What is this blackbird doing, singing all night long,
night after night, as if deceived by streetlight?
Urban blackbirds should have worked it out by now:
the night is not the real McCoy in town,
but lesser day, prolonged by artifice.

Perhaps the ancient Manichaean blackbird brain
commanding song or silence, forced in modern times
to bathe in pools of compromising light by night,
has, under Darwin's laws, adapted and evolved
into a shades-of-greybird brain today.

This blackbird likes to party, never mind the hour.
Its stamina has kept me nightly company
and neither it nor I is worried that, at dawn,
when, as I used to think, God cries, 'Cue blackbird!',
it and I may well, displeasing God, have gone to sleep.

# Aloft

The unison of wing beat as the birds take off,
to wheel in hundreds, linked by silent knowledge,
leaving me standing, face up, wondering
why, and why now, and how do they all know?

# Car Wash

I'm at the car wash with six cars in front of me. I have the radio.
   No hurry.

Twenty minutes later, I approach the outside gang.
Four men converge with sponges, heavy-duty soap and purple squirt
   for hubcaps.
For a time I can't see out. I'm in a shady, trusting world of grey-
   white bubbles.

Pressure hoses douse me clean. The outside windscreen gleams.
   The usual line the windscreen wiper leaves has disappeared.
The voices of the men are Eastern European. That is all I know.
The one who does the corner by the driver's door looks in.
   'All right!' he shouts.
I give an upward nod, and smile.

Now I advance towards the inside gang.
They'll vacuum the seats and carpets, Windolene the inside glass,
   spray fake fruit-blossom polish on the fascias.
I get out and stand aside and look around.

An *Evening Standard* article, proclaiming this 'The Best Hand Job in
   London', has been stuck up on the office door.
Across the ceiling of the shed are zig-zag lines of plastic Union Jacks.
I shout, 'All right!' whenever someone shouts, 'All right!' at me.

The boss comes to collect a ten-pound note. I give him two pounds
   more.
'The lads!' I shout. He thanks me. Then he stops, and listens.
   'What is that?'

The music from my radio, released through all five open doors, is
    climbing over held high notes of vacuum cleaners, bass of traffic
    hum, the intervening cries of work.

'Dvorák!' I answer. Slight pause. 'Czech composer!' 'Yes,' he shouts,
    'I know!'
We stand and pay attention to a rising tune on violins,
repeated. Somewhere, something is remembered, out of reach.
He looks at me. His face is working. Then he turns his head.

The men have finished and they put the music back into its box.
They signal that they're ready for the next.

# In a Station of the Underground

The young man, dreadlocked, in his too blue uniform
is reading Homer.

The night wind splashes rain across an empty concourse
to his cabin door.

Five minutes till the last train comes.  His shift
is almost over

and, judging by the pages he's got left,
he's nearing Ithaca.

# Embracing on Escalators

Couples travelling on escalators are more likely to embrace
(whether they're teenage lovers or old flames or just husbands
     and wives)
than when they're standing on the pavement or in a park or at some
     other level place.

There are two reasons for this.  First, escalators offer to their over-
     busy lives
a non-optional and prolonged pause (as long as they stand on
     the right):
a reminder that the hopeful traveller is happier than the traveller
     who arrives.

Secondly, many loving and faithful couples are of uneven height.
For them, love-making in bed, depending on the position they
     like best,
may not involve much facial contact, whatever its genital delight,

with one face squashed uncomfortably against the other's heaving
     chest,
the other buried in a pillow, keeping going with blocked airways and
     sightless eyes.
(Despite these disadvantages, such couples often achieve climax, and
     afterwards rest.)

Even the public shows of affection which lovers of mismatched size
allow themselves on pavements or in parks or at other level places
     must employ
stooping and stretching movements, physical strains which compromise

---

the pleasure in embracing which equal-statured couples can enjoy.
But on the escalator, all is changed! For once neither low nor high,
these erstwhile awkward partners see a different girl, a different boy,

a new angel! They are the favoured ones now. Around them, north
    and south, fly
other pairs of carnal angels at the same unhurried pace,
each on an equal footing as mouth encounters mouth and eye
    meets eye.

# Tribute

*In memoriam Sue Goldie, 1939–2010*

'My golden girl has gone.' Mike gave me that first line
the Monday morning when he phoned. The afternoon before
she'd travelled quietly beyond us. In his voice
I heard the full acknowledgement of absence, loss.

No poem, eulogy, not music even is equipped
to make of absence, presence; to restore the loss.
We're here to bolster with our love those most bereft,
and with what instruments we have, to say:

'We knew a woman rare in beauty, great of heart.
No truer spirit of conviviality
inhabited the earth; no one more open-handedly
imparted gladness. She was laughter given flesh.

Sister, mother, lover, wife and friend:
she lived life as intended, to our benefit;
and children in their thousands whom she taught
are living tributes walking in the world today.'

If memory needs something physical to cling to, it could be:
her eyes, in which the light of holiday was always shining;
or her hair, an outward glory of her nature, which was golden.

## 'For this Relief, Much Thanks'

High-minded, gloomy critics have been heard to say
that modern poetry's descended to the sewer;
that poets courting popularity today
fill up their lines with matter noxious and obscure.
This lyric will confirm those Jeremiahs' fears
in praising Bazalgette, the prince of engineers.

Noble Sir Joseph: every time I flush the loo
I fondly think of you, whose genius has meant
that I'm not wading daily in a foetid brew
expelled from London's bladder and its fundament.
Shit happens, as it must; your tunnels have embraced
our city's Stygian floods of stinking human waste.

We rightly laud the works of Barry, Scott or Wren,
whose towers, domes and spires connect us to the sky;
yet sturdy structures hidden from the eyes of men
may stand and serve the public good as worthily.
Grand, soaring buildings should arouse our proper pride
but calls of nature cannot meanwhile be denied.

Wren's famous epitaph we know: 'If you require
a monument, look round' – a great man's lofty boast,
commanding us – us lesser mortals – to admire.
Too modest is the tribute to Sir Joseph's ghost:
'Flumini vincula posuit' imperfectly explains
the debt we owe to his two thousand miles of drains.

His shrine by the Embankment should, in stone, have said:
'He banished squalor, put to flight the noisome stench
of piss and ordure. And he marked a watershed;
the Thames is now a river, not a toilet trench.
From death by cholera he rescued London Town.
If monument you seek, you Londoners, look down!'

# Cross-channel Ferry

*'Il connut la mélancolie des paquebots.'*

A husband sat at dinner with his wife
and watched the passage of the level sea.
The girl who served them served his fantasy:
tight skirt, white shirt, the *à la* schoolgirl tie.
She knew she could disarm him with her smile,
and did, and still did later as he queued
to buy his wife her half-expected gift:
the perfume she assured him that she loved.

Outside the shop, he stood and tried to peel
the price off cleanly with his fingernail.
A woman of his age was watching him:
the incomplete, well-meaning English male.
He caught her knowing eye. Its sympathy
provoked his laughter and a train of thought:

*We mostly don't get what we want. But then*
*fidelity is best. But time is short*
*and lust at sixty is lust none the less*
*for being futile, and ridiculous.*

## She who had Loved Horses

She who had loved horses knew her time had come
and now, as she lay dying, the last two in her keeping,
who would outlive her, as they knew, came sidling
up the back field, as they never did, to the window to stand
and attend her spirit until it leapt beyond
them and the place and took its straight line to the sun.

# Desolate

She tries to strike with him the flint of eyes.
He makes sure to withhold from her his glance.
Each occupies a separate dull place
and their free actions brought them to this pass.

They chose to marry, chose to speak the words,
repeated as it were a playground verse
whose questions and replies are sound, not sense,
to be unspoken without consequence.

She knows this, as she contemplates her loss,
alone in the spare room, gazing at space.
The lack of tenderness, the want of joy:
no heartless social law took these away.

She knows this, and the knowledge is the pain;
no one to call on, no one else to blame.

# Offspring

The first was born at midnight in July
of 1946, and there was peace.
She lay beside a window in the ward
and saw the dawn, and heard a blackbird sing.
The light grew stronger and the stillness held.
Her future beckoned; she would shape her world.

For those who will insist too stridently
time's languid humour keeps its own redress.
She loved her children, and they came to know
her stringent sets of measures of success
which, over fifty years, all failed to match.
They made their way in life by minor roads.
Most married wrongly, and she had to watch.
The Gospel she had taught them – which for her
contained the full sufficiency of truth
for here and for hereafter – most denied.

A blackbird sings at daybreak this July.
In bed at home, she still invests with hope
the sweet, the automatic line of notes
speaking to her in age as plausibly
as when the song said: 'Time is on your side.'

# The Twelfth of July

The holidays are here, most of his friends
have got away to France or Italy
to do the things that holidaying people do
in countries which gave up religious wars some time ago.

But he's stayed on, patiently living through
the build-up to the rite of dominance
enacted every *belle saison* on this side of the waters.
He'll take a break in Donegal in August.

Now, of an afternoon of heat, he's driving home
at ease in the lanes he knows, an elbow out the window,
until he meets a road-block manned by boys.
He slows and stops. One juts his head in. 'Name and business, mister?'

This mister's business, all his life, has been
to fetch and carry ordinary hope from side to side,
to take down barriers a notch, a notch.
The words form in his mind, 'Get out the fucking road
or else…' But one says, 'Let him pass, hi.
The oul' fella walks the dog across his field.'
They drop the rope and shift an oil drum.

                          Driving on,
the thought which hurts him with a hurt he'll have to overcome
is that his neighbours' children have the confidence
to strut with sticks and challenges the land he shares;
that prisoners of history so narrowly confined
can be so sure they speak and act as freed men.

Big day today for boys not going anywhere.
Big night tonight, the highlight of their year:
a bonfire on a bit of tarmac outside Antrim.

# At Cross Keys

*To Peter Logue*

Just when we thought we'd leave, the penny whistle started it
and all of us who'd been half hoping all the evening
turned our chairs half round and paid attention.

The main event – two flutes, a banjo and a bodhrán –
kept it up, unflagging, for three hours.  In between each tune
a quick discussion, nodding of the heads, and on.

Ice on the roads outside.  Mist rising from the Bann.
Within, the curtains closed, the coal fire leaping
and the whole thing happening unplanned

yet riding on consent between the players and the listeners,
the compact we had entered into, there and then:
acknowledging a rarity the room contained.

It broke up about two, with handshakes, hearty thanks.
The drink was in me.  I could hear myself.
My English accent felt like nakedness.

Peter, thank God you knew the place.  Thank God we ventured out
to seek a bit of music on a Saturday.
The night's coincidences added up to grace.

# The Least You Can Say

What was there to say at the wake
when the man in the coffin on view
(the coffin lid propped at the wall)
had had, as the mourners well knew,
no virtues to speak of at all?
What minimum tribute to make?

No guest in the house felt inspired
to bestow on the dead, who, in life,
had been bigoted, humourless, mean,
harsh on his children, cold to his wife,
now thankfully passed from the scene,
the praise that good manners required.

The silence weighs down like a cloak
but for coughing and shifting of feet,
each visitor dumb where he sits;
till a neighbour gets up from his seat
for a cigarette. 'Well,' he admits,
'he certainly knew how to smoke.'

# The Lake Poets

There's a certain sort of poetry whose production I'd love to curb:
the sort that gets written at venues where the surroundings are truly
    superb.

At Annaghmakerrig in Monaghan they run all kinds of courses
for artists in need of a pick-me-up for their failing inner resources.

The landscape is stunning for miles around, with lakes and drumlins
    a-plenty:
it's just the job for the journeyman whose tank is running on empty.

My friend took a party of teachers there for a session of in-service
    training.
The weather wasn't so great that day; it was misty and cold and
    raining.

It was all going well when a man burst in – the manager, visibly
    stressed;
he was sorry to interrupt the course, but he had an urgent request:

'Does anyone own a red Vauxhall? Would you move it, for Jesus'
    sake?
I've a roomful of poets next door. It's blocking their view of the lake.'

# Hares at Aldegrove Airport

An early flight from London on a crystal day in March.
The English coast near Liverpool, the Isle and Calf of Man,
the Irish coast by Strangford Lough. A change of engine note,
the swift descent across the little fields, Lough Neagh ahead,
a bump, the sharp deceleration, taxi to the runway's end,
a U-turn, taxi back toward the terminal.

My luck to have a starboard window seat.
Indifferent, it seemed, to aircraft and their noise,
a dozen hares were boxing on the grass between the runways.

Hares were carriers of light for Eostre, goddess of the dawn.
She gave her name to Easter.
On the full moon stands a hare who holds an egg.
The females biff the males.

All useful background. But to see them there, that morning,
going at it just as they're supposed to: wonder was enough.

# A Gift from David Hammond

David Hammond gave me this one day: the night before,
he'd attended a wake. It was all carried on
as tradition required: the open coffin, the handshakes,
the quiet sad words, tea and whiskey and bread and butter.
Except that, as the centre of attention,
the deceased had competitors: two bonny baby boys, twins,
in a double pram, their shy proud parents standing either side.
An excess of cooing and clucking, admiration,
approval of the given names, until an old farmer,
who had managed cattle all his life, approached.
'Boys, are they?' he asked the father, who smiled and nodded.
And the old man followed up with, 'D'you plan on keeping both
    of them?'

# Quintet

Applause. The players sit, and settle. Pause. And then
a quick acknowledgement of eyebrows, and begin.

It always takes a while for time to leave the room:
for music only, and its makers, to remain.

But leave it does, and here, I see, first cello
wears a beatific smile, as if possessed by ghosts
of genius inhabiting her trembling fingers,
visitors unbidden whom she gladly hosts.

Schubert's String Quintet in C is serious:
first violin has worked her face into a frown,
prising the clearest truth she can from lines of code.
The five unite, the one divides, and we are one

with them, within the music, in the silences
the other side of music. In their give-and-go,
their nods and glances, each one guards apartness
and surrenders to entirety. And this is how

they turn our various, distracted minds, and lead them,
willing and intent for now, deep, deeper, down
swimming in wells of sound at once familiar
and, as they plumb the furthest mysteries, unknown.

# Frosterley Marble

Ralph Walton mines at Frosterley six days a week.
The seventh day he rests, which means he travels far
to preach the Word of God to fellow Methodists.
'God made the world and all that's in it in six days.'
At work on Monday, Ralph, his brothers and his cousins
prise galena from the earth – their daily bread –
until they come by chance upon a rarity,
a welcome bonus to their earnings from the lead:
a slab of marble. Hacked out, trundled to the surface,
brushed and washed, the piece encases, white on black,
the fossilised remains of creatures of the sea.
Ralph stands and wonders. I am wondering today
at scores of *Dibunophylum bipartitum,*
the specimens held fast for millions of years
in this now polished artefact at Stanhope,
up the road from where Ralph named their find 'the cockle post'.
Total abstainer, literate, he knows his Bible.
Why would God have planted cockles underground?
Across his mind there floats the shadow of a doubt,
like darkening clouds on Weardale in the spring
which interrupt the gift of sunshine that he loves
and (barring Sundays on the road) sees little of.

# 4

# Snake by the River

Swimming upstream, in the deep part they have dammed,
I am a white fish nosing and breasting,
largest and noisiest of the river animals,
with distinctive bum which bounces up and down.

At such well publicised approach, the other creatures
minutes ago found hideouts in the weeds
and now they squat there, silently wondering
while the commotion incautiously proceeds.

Only, on a low scoop of willow branch to water,
unperturbed, and hanging in the medium between
the branch and the stream, the green bank
and the leaf-shadowed air, here is a green snake,

looped and lank, careless as the afternoon,
careless who passes, what their purposes.
By acknowledgement, he unhooks an eye, one.
Three times the tongue moves; each within time's merest section.

The white fish abandons his disguise, stands
up to his thighs in the river, and a moment
of pure surprise, of frank, transparent fear,
shocking like new cold water, overflows him.

The string of bubbles from the mud around his feet,
the Malaga-Madrid, shrieking across fields,
a man who passes singing on his bike
invade the moment, fix it, it is now,

it is done. But, for a moment, the water,
handling the white thighs of the standing man,
has linked him to the body of the snake
where it dips its curl of smudged green inches in

and, when the human stare and the snake's eye
meet in the air, the moment's tension
has held them both still, as mutually they weigh
their sense of danger, and of recognition.

# Familiarity Need Not Breed Contempt

Man and woman come and go together
over the field and around the house
for a full hour every evening.

Their tasks are fixed. He attends to the pig;
she is to and fro with buckets from the river
for watering the flowers.

His back to her, lifting and stooping, speaks familiarity
and when he turns he will see her back
bent over tin cans of geraniums
and now and then his glance encounters hers.
But they are business-like, and do not linger.

Once only, I heard laughter and caught them
between the red blooms, in the corner by the door.
He waited over her, mocking and calling
with high-voiced, sung words, over and over.
She, half humoured, made as if to go, yet still
drew the moment out, expectant,
faltering between the man who waited, and the flowers.

# Sketches in Andalucía

## Mountain Drive at Night

The horses stand lop-limbed and grey in the depth of the night.
They graze at the summits of mountain passes
where pasture is scabby and where few come.

Their heads, attentive for a moment to our lights,
their hollow sides, the angles of their bones, are ancient.
These harsh lines were drawn in ochre on cave walls.

Their silence and stillness are deeper than to be dazzled
by bright velocity which races where the years have stayed.

## Stones at Ronda la Vieja

Some centuries ago, men gathered up these stones
in great white heaps, to clear a field.

Some centuries before, the Romans came
to slaughter and subject
and when the necessary blood had stained the ground
to sit back on this height, survey this new patch of their map,
these miles of blond dry earth and olives, sunlit empty distances.

What had they come to conquer?

Still, they sharpened swords, bred exiles, built a theatre.
We send our speeches to the tiers of seats
where grass cushions a long play.
The fashioned stones repeat. We speak again. Repeat.

A man has stopped two horses and a wooden plough
between the dry earth and the damp, halfway along a furrow.
He is absent. Noon and silence. Staring at the ground, the horses,
patient, motionless,
attend the man's return
to haul his brief damp trail through broken Roman stones.

## New Calf

You wonder how, two hours ago
such a beast of muscle and bone
got out of his mother
without gashing her wider.

She leans her long side against the wall
breathing and resentful.
Afterbirth, membrane and blood
hang to the ground.

She wishes no more of this burden.
When he leans under to suck,
unpractised, he bites.
She kicks with her knee.

The farmer interposes his morality
thumps the cow
holds the calf's head so he sucks gently.

Her eyes are large with the indignity.

# We Came with the Rain

*Triacastela, province of Lugo, Spain*

We came with the rain
down from the hills where nobody came
to the market-day crowd in the village, quick openings of umbrellas,
wet faces calling over the street,
crowding into bar entrances, doorways,
the whole place jangling with the people and the storm.

Inside the bar, all tables occupied, they talked.
But *talked* says nothing of
that leaning into each other with hope,
lavish in utterance, equal in response.
We shouted for our drinks
and watched the room fill with the sound

and then we left.
We were fast-moving people in a place
where value is retained
who had a programme of our own construction for the day
who let our own inertia override,
which I regret.

The afternoon has left, indelible in memory,
those faces, laughing, rained on,
exalted in communion; and then an eagle, up the road an hour,
back among high hills and in sunlight,
who, startled in his steady occupation of the air,
moved up a gear, and up, and out of sight.

# Beside the Sea, the Sea

Thessaloniki –
March sunshine and the slap of water on the wharf.
The sea is full of fish, in swift grey shoals,
right here, below me. And the same sea
is full of filth as well: oil slicks, sewage, cola cans.

Aegean, myth-bearer, what a state of shame we've brought you to,
slopping our mess, sporting our brand names!
Aegeus in his grief would not have thrown himself in here.

To make amends for this gross injury
we face a Heraklean task, yet one
within our common capability:
we clean up our act. Placate Poseidon. Hope to God
the shoals of swift grey fish hang in there till we do.
If not (it is no myth) – catastrophe.

# Animal Rescue Squad

*To Paul Halley*

To begin with an apology, other poets
have told of animals they'd found at night on roads,
dead, wounded or frightened, and of what they did.
As subject matter it comes ready made
and dangerous for that: an open goal, easy to miss.

Nonetheless. Three a.m., a Massachusetts country road,
the black heap in the headlights is a foal, collapsed.
The two of us get out and, nervous of country things,
we study it, we fear its legs are broken.
To our relief it stands up. It falls down again.
It is terrified of us, of what has happened,
and then we work out what has happened.

Thirty feet of steep and muddy bank above the road
a stallion and a mare rush in anxiety
behind a fence which leaves a foal-sized gap
between the barbed wire and the sloping ground.

There is the problem. Something quickly should be done
in case a truck comes charging round the bend
the other way, without the stretch of straight road we have had.
Maybe we should wake the farmer. Here I make
one more apology, to Massachusetts farmers,
I am sure a gentle kind of men
but stereotypes are powerful at night
and films we've seen about America
have snarling dogs and shotguns blazing down the drive.
Better to face the horses.

                                    But a foal is quite a weight.
We heave it upright, haul it off the road,
point it at the bank. In no mood to co-operate,
it acts the awkward baby, determined to fall down.

The method of ascent: man A has the animal
by the belly, proffered forward and upward. Man B
is pushing at the haunch and fetlocks of man A.
Soon our casual wear is all messed up, man A tastes grass,
the octoped, hard breathing and backsliding, mounts.

Mare and stallion have been watching this
and he is frantic, straining at the wire.
Disaster threatens if he breaks the fence.
But the posts hold, we get within his reach,
his long head comes at me and I am glad
to feel his tongue apply its sputum to my face and hair.

We're not there yet, because the foal for once
refuses to fall down beside the wire.
We push it over, shovel it under,
and still it needs another lift and stagger
to the flat bit in the middle of the field.
Effusive is the right word for the stallion's thanks now,
lathering me further; but the mare is circumspect.
The smell of strangers on her young is strong.

Men A and B hold onto one another
and their unfit hearts hurt. Emergencies like that
don't happen every night, and we are glad our headlights
found the creature first, not just because a truck,
taking the bend now, breaks the silence and the dark.

# As Anacondas Go

The anaconda is regarding me from up that tree
with merely intellectual interest. The enormous bulge
which quadruples its girth part way along the heaps of coils
which occupy the sagging branches of the tree is proof.
An anaconda isn't one for snacking between meals.
Obesity is not a risk it runs. Our guide would guess
it won't be in a mood for eating for at least a week.
'What does it eat?' I ask. 'Oh, meat in general,' he says,
'though probably' – he sizes up my lanky frame – 'not you.
You'd be too big. It's only small as anacondas go.'

Our very small canoe makes progress through the flooded grove.
I'm glad I'm big as tourists go. I'm hoping not to meet
an anaconda here who's hungry and who isn't small
as anacondas go. The guide has brought a hunting knife
which is, I see, quite big as weapons go for self-defence.
My wish not to be squeezed out of my middle-sized dear life
is, out of all proportion to the way things go, immense.

# Voyeur

I'm drinking on the terrace of a hotel in Bangkok.
Across the street, six girls are lounging, laughing in a flock,
sure to command attention and prepared to advertise.
Beyond my strength, the self-denial to avert the eyes
and so, in those rare moments when no traffic's in the way,
I gaze in admiration at the talent on display.
Sweet birds of youth, this flirting hour the street is your domain;
don't mind an old spectator who's got beauty on the brain.

# The Interior Life of Insects

The house is full of insects, arrived by accident
through open doors and windows,
up drainpipes, between floorboards, down the chimney.

Once in, they are diminished, out of the element
which set their brains aflutter
and drove them, until now unquestioning, to do or die.

Soldiers astray, lacking commanders, some set forth on silent
route marches over featureless walls,
their hopeless mission: to regain known territory.

Others stand immobilised for hours at a fixed point
in a trance of indecision,
the print of information fading from the memory.

In all of them, sooner or later, fuel and force are spent,
they drop down and disintegrate
and get swept up. Always the last to fall, the manic fly

launches and relaunches for its proper continent,
draining its reserves of energy
to make the light the air, its day lucky.

# Chapel of Rest

*In memoriam Albert Penhouët, 1931-2004*

I never saw you, living, in a suit, my dear old friend
and here you lie, all buttoned up in single-breasted beige,
white shirt, dark tie, prepared by other hands to say goodbye.

Your own hands – builder's, gardener's hands – show forth their
    healed-up cuts
and calluses to contradict the attitude of prayer
they've been forced into to console us that you've gone somewhere.

You had no truck with that. For you, to work was not to pray.
I found you harvesting potatoes one Assumption Feast
and made a joke about you working on a day of rest.

You stopped, and said, 'I don't believe. I never go to church.
In my philosophy we're born, we grow up, fall in love,
we work, enjoy ourselves, and help the people we can reach.

We hope to live a good long time. That's it. And then we die.
The spuds are small this year. Too little rain in May and June.
But it'll make them tasty. Bring the barrow over here.'

Today, no object in the room commemorates that speech.
The crucifix and candles offer comfortable lies
in case we can't abide the truth you faced with open eyes.

# Evening Swim

I throw myself into the sea, for joy.
The crowds have gone.
These shallows hold the day's heat.
Properly afloat, I point myself into the rush and roar of waves.
I know and override the reflex fear,
emerge into the colder, darker water
where the proper swimming starts:
a steady breast stroke. Take a breath. Head under for two strokes,
and up, and breathe, and under for two strokes, and out and out.

I stop and turn to face the shore.
How distant seems the playtime fuss of breakers here.
How even more remote my solitary car, across the beach, above the
    dunes.
The grown-up ocean thrills and carries me.
I'm strong. I've been this far before. I'm tiny in the deep.

The inward swim, the same procedure: arms and legs
are confidently forcing water backwards, minute after minute.
Stop again. I'm tired now, and breathing hard.
The waves, the shore, the dunes, the car
have all stayed where they were.

Trust to your strength. Increase the rate. Head under for two
    strokes,
and up, and breathe, and under for two strokes…
I'm spending energy so limbs and lungs are burning
but no progress. I am far from joy, as cold and doubt approach me.
Am I strong? What is this unaccustomed feeling
as my body loses power and my breath is ugly snoring

from a mouth so stretched to gaping that I swallow water
and its sour arrival makes my stomach flinch?

Try not to panic. Stop once more. Cease swimming for a while.
Perhaps a shoreward drift will catch you, reel you in.

That life could end this easily.
He died of carelessness.
Police, alerted, found the little pile of clothes, the towel, the car key.
    Obvious.
Informed the next of kin.
Increased by one the count of summer drownings.
Later, down the coast, the sea coughed up a pustulating mess.

I hang there, waiting on the sea's caprice,
out of my element and mortally alone,
my fellow humans – all six billion of them – elsewhere.

The day I learnt to read.
My birth year and my death year on a stone.
The time I held her in a field of sunflowers.
The time I made her angry and she ran along the shore ahead of me.

Perhaps the shore is closer than it was?
Encouraged, I begin to swim again. This time I'm travelling.
Relief adds purchase to my strokes.
Head under, one stroke, two strokes, up again and breathe. And in
    and in.

I'm near the waves, I'm in their gravity,
one covers me, it spins me round,
I'm happy to be helpless as my head hits sand.
The wave recedes. I try to stand. The next one knocks me down.
I stand again and, stumbling, gain the land.

---

Bent over, hands on knees, I puke up water, groaning,
empty but of gratitude. The pride is out of me.

The footprints from the shoreline to my clothes: unsteady, wandering.
These seabirds are my only witnesses.
I dry and dress myself, and climb the wooden steps up to the road.

I open all the windows of the greenhouse car
and head for home. The pride is sneaking in.
Ascending through the gears, I plan my story
as the blessed breeze I might have missed is ruffling my hair
and crystallising salt on sun-tanned skin:
'I did enjoy my swim. The sea was warm. The waves were fun.'

## Vacheries

'How are you keeping, double four nine five?'

'One mustn't grouse as long as one's alive.
I know it's only milk that we produce,
but still one likes to feel that one's of use.
It's better now the cooler weather's here.
Don't you agree, four two eight three my dear,
that summer is unbearable? The flies,
disgusting creatures, crawling in our eyes;
the dry grass, tasteless; no shade in the field;
and then the farmer moans about our yield!
He's just a brute, that man, all take take take;
and stingy, with his low-grade cattle cake –
an insult. When it comes to quality
I know a thing or two. He can't fool me.

You see poor four six nine eight over there?
Don't say I told you this: she's in despair
and here's the reason – it's a frightful shame.
This morning, when our lord and master came,
he found her number badge and bent her ear.
I heard him tell her (I was standing near):
"If you don't pull your socks up and lactate,
I see your future on a dinner plate."
Can you imagine it? So coarse! So rude!
I'm not surprised it's put her off her food.
She says her life's just not worth living now.
She'd rather get it over with, poor cow.

What can one do? The bar code doesn't lie.
She's heading for that cowshed in the sky.
One can't but feel a certain sympathy.

And how's life treating you, four two eight three?'

## Vacheries en français

*À mon cher ami Dominique Gragnic,*
*qui n'est pas le fermier dans ce poème*

« Salut! Comment vas-tu, quat' cinq neuf six? »
« On est en vie, au moins.  On rend service.
On donne son lait chaque jour.  C'est quelque chose.
On ne peut pas se plaindre, je suppose.
Ça va mieux par ce temps d'automne plus frais.
Je trouve l'été insupportable, tu sais,
avec ces mouches malpropres infestant
nos yeux; puis l'absence d'ombre dans le champ;
l'herbe fade; et – comble de désagrément –
un paysan qui conteste notr' rendement!
Ce n'est qu'une brute, cet homme, un malhonnête.
Et tu as vu le tourteau qu'il nous jette?
Dégoûtant, dernière des qualités.
Mais pas si bête; il n'va pas me tromper.

Viens plus près, ma chère, regarde là-bas.
La pauvre double quat' neuf cinq – tu vois?
Ne dis rien aux autres, je te prie.
Elle ne prend plus de plaisir à la vie.
Et tu connais la cause?  C'est scandaleux.
L'autr' jour est venu cet homme odieux,
a pris son badge et tiré son oreille.
J'étais à côté.  Il l'a menacée!
– *Ou tu augmentes ta production de lait*
*ou tu vas chez Bigard en steacks hachés.*
– Non, mais tu t'imagines!  C'est d'un vulgaire!
Un manque extrême de politesse, ma chère.

---

Elle ne mange pas. Tu vois comme elle maigrit?
Son existence n'est plus qu'une agonie.
Que faire?  Le code-barres ne saurait mentir.
Ses jours sont comptés.  Elle veut en finir.
Une vacherie l'attend au paradis.
N'éprouve-t-on pas une certaine sympathie?

Et toi, quat' deux trois sept, ça va, la vie? »

# The Squirrels and the Nut Trees

Red squirrels here in Brittany are shy.
But I saw five at once the other day
engaged in brazen daylight robbery.

The walnuts and the hazelnuts were ripe.
The squirrels got at them by aerial leap
from overhanging oaks, bridging a gap

which you would think required the power of flight.
Never a false move. Every judgment right.
A season's harvest picked off, fruit by fruit,

to be secreted in the neighbour's wood.
And I, indulgent victim of this raid,
am rich in nut trees, poor in nuts, and glad.

# Cut Cornfield

Stop at the gap as you pass, and size up the field.
Its shape is not a figure in geometry.
To follow its containing bank – bushes and trees
atop the others' work of raised-up earth and stones –
would be a half-hour walk. At this time yesterday
it held its yield of barley, grey with readiness.
The combines lit and cut the crop all night, droning
and ceasing at the edge of earshot in our dreams.
The bailers crossed the same ground all today, and now
the evening sees me counting up the rounded bails,
tight in their plastic, spaced and settled where they dropped.
Beyond a hundred, I lose sight and count of them
in distance and the shallow water of the sun.
The men have gone to spend their Saturday; machines
to cool and click in yards. The local moment lasts
until I break it, and drive on. The others stay,
unhurried, on eternal holiday, to watch
the failing sunlight and the rounding of the moon.

# Partridges in September

These partridges, released on Tuesday
so that men on Sundays now the autumn's here
can mooch about and shoot them,
must, after months of cosseted confinement,
be – what? terrified? exhilarated? baffled?
They precede me on the road, putting a brave face on it,
an urgent delegation late for an appointment.
I slow the car to walking pace.
They quicken theirs, but slightly; dignity's to be preserved.
We could be here all morning. I've been here before.
It's only when their walk becomes a trot
and then a scamper, frankly fugitive,
that they will take the aerial route to save themselves.
Have centuries of firearms taught them
that they're safer on the ground?
I'm in no hurry, and a minute passes
as my silly anxious escort runs before the chariot.
At last I've had enough; a change of engine note, my gathering speed,
and up they rise, compelled to demonstrate
a risky, last-ditch talent which you sense they'd rather hide.

# An Argument of Fowls

The great gold crane presides an empty building site
this evening as the light fails.  On its overreaching arm,
locked until morning, gather starlings in their thousands, each
a separated dot of black,
finding its own place on the fretwork,
plain to see against the backlit wash of sky.

Collective noun for starlings?  Fifty years ago
I learnt it as a truth as solid as
the capital of Ecuador, the crops
principally grown in Thailand and Cambodia,
the product of twelve twelves.

                        A murmuration.
And a source of wonderment, that word!
Its length.  Its difference from its duller fellows – herds and flocks.
The teacher loved it too.  It was her chance
to lead us boldly into criticism, aided by a term
yet more exotic, liquid on the tongue
and bound to feature in the spelling test next week:
that *murmuration* was a case of onomatopoeia
was as sure as Quito.

                      *The Boke of Saint Albans,*
printed 1486, collects the phrase (with scores of others,
as 'a Cherme of Goldefynches', 'an Exaltying of Larkis').
It uses the old form 'stares' for starlings.
We children didn't know how many centuries had passed
since starlings first had been supposed to murmur as the night
      comes on.

And yet the evidence I hear this evening, as the night comes on,
is contrary: not murmuring – that quiet conversation of familiars –
but angry squawking in the way antagonists
will interrupt each other's sentences, their voices
climbing over one another, bullying the audience,
insisting on the satisfaction of the final word.

Will this – I fall back on the default noun (the duller fellow)
for a group of birds – will this great flock of starlings
take advantage of the steady, leafless, metal bough
extended from a sudden trunk
to roost in, high above the planes and sycamores?

I have my answer in the almost dark.
Collective nouns (those friends I used to think that I could trust)
may fail me, but collective memory – the unschooled,
common mental property of crowds – endures.
The animals make wing down to the trees in clouds.

# After Frost's 'After Apple-Picking'

'My [lightweight, three-piece] ladder's sticking through a tree
Toward heaven still'
and Robert Frost and I
have these two things in common: we write (he wrote) poetry
and we have (he had) apples by the ton.
Saint Martin's summer's sun
has blessed my harvesting, and now illuminates
dozens of wooden boxes, plastic crates
dotted round the orchard on the hill
and left until tomorrow to be barrowed in and stored.
Like him, I'm glad,
in a way, to see the business over with, to be allowed to stop.
One can get bored
admiring each warm, individual beauty in a massive crop.
He said he had
'ten thousand thousand' grade-one fruit;
in other words, ten million – a figure I'd dispute
but poets will and should exaggerate.
We've both had vintage years, at any rate.
And now the problem starts;
it's always like this when a bumper season ends.
How many apples can I palm off on my friends,
make chutney of, turn into pies and tarts?
How long, oh Lord (till Christmas?) must we eat stewed apple (laced,
I will admit, with Calvados)
at lunch and dinner every day
in order not to feel a sense of loss
that one of your free gifts has gone to waste?

It is, I know, effrontery
to bracket in a poem Robert Frost and me.
But let the minor poet have his say.
Robert, your talent is the ripest specimen a summer's light achieves.
I'm up the ladder, on the topmost rung. It's out of reach.
Mine's green and runtish, low down, hidden in the leaves.
Yet we are each
wealthy this evening as we sit and write indoors.
Sleep well tonight, 'whatever sleep it is'. One final piece of cheek:
I bet you, any day this sunlit week,
I've handled apples just as big as yours.

# In Cléguer Cemetery

Here in an avenue of stones
Algeria's local veterans
take leave of one of theirs.
In not quite military lines
they stand, flags dipped. The priest intones
appropriate rapid prayers.

Though matters of small note have filled
the peaceful years since they were called
to make light of their lives,
in these who did as they were told
when young and strong, the stubborn pride
of fellowship survives.

The coffin slots into its grave.
Old men are harder to deceive.
They know they lost that futile war.
They furl the flags and seek the bar.

# The Plough

The night is clear.  I'm looking up
at seven stars which form a group,
the first my father pointed out:
'Those are the Plough.' Which they were not,
as well I knew, but metaphors
are good for recognising stars.

Until today I didn't know
that some stars making up the Plough
are further from each other than
they are from us – our earth, our sun.
From someone out there's point of view
we're in a constellation too.

What other trigonometry
do they employ to map the sky?
How must our glimmer look to them
and by what reassuring name
might they in metaphor relate
their handled world to spots of light?

# Bright Eyes

The owl that calls and calls and, pausing, calls again
is speaking to me, as I fancy, lying here,
the bedroom and its furniture made pale and strange
by patination borrowed from a hanging moon.

How lovely the night is!  Creeping out of bed,
I pad downstairs, open the door, and stand like Adam
on the spiky lawn, where dew is gathering.
Somewhere, at the edge of earshot, under lights,
a combine makes short work of one more wheat field.
Stars are myriad but shy, outfaced by moonlight,
as the bird who summoned me repeats herself
once, twice – 'to-wit, to-wit' – then hesitates,
suspicious of a foreign presence on her ground.

A minute passes.  Now the overarching oak
releases her, my fellow vigilant,
bright-eyed Athena, wings outstretched,
who sails straight by my upturned wondering face
and down the silver valley till I've lost her
and I wait, and then… 'to-wit, to-wit… to-wit'
as Adam shivers with a sense of benefit.

# Wind-blown Acanthus

The man was nearly blind; in six months would be dead.
I led him to the decorated chapel door.
Five hundred years had worked to soften and abrade
the clean, sharp patterns chased there by the mason's blade.
He knew his stuff, though; with enquiring hands he read
the granite and, greeting an old friend's face once more
after long absence, 'Wind-blown acanthus,' he said.

## Short and Sweet

October's here; it's time for fond farewells
to these I've gorged on all too briefly in September:
golden mirabelles.

# A Kingfisher in August

Swim down towards the bridge for half an hour.
Stillness and heat are in this green river.
Your mind is free. Now flip onto your back
to see the alders, leaning from the bank,
descending to you. Close your eyes. The leaves
print shadows on the light behind the lids.
The river bends, the children's voices
playing on the sandbank now are hushed.
There is only you, and a breeze in the alders
to tell you something you already know
about an older and a calmer world
than that you move in most months of the year.
Pay the breeze attention while you drift and float.
The office babble of July regains
full volume in September. Listen and
you won't hear either. You are out of reach.

Summer has prevailed at last, and in this state
of solo contemplation, suddenly
you have an escort in a blur of wings:
midnight in daylight. Back and forth he skims,
adornment, outrider; and the bird men used
to hunt, stop up and murder in his hole
is now your guarantee of passage
on the river, your free right to drift and float.

And when you reach the bridge, he's with you still,
your own wild mascot, as you stand and shake
the water from your skin, and feel the sun
burn your good flesh. Here they won't come looking
for you or for him. Now they can't touch us.

# The River

Impossible to verify its one and only source:
a trickle here, a darker patch there in the grass
in upland country, on a bald plateau,
a trace squeezed out of rock, the mountain's bulk.

It may be, once, that transhumancing shepherds knew.
There is a place, a mile or two below its origin,
where one might say for certain, 'This is it.
This is the course to which the other courses
will contribute, will be tributaries,'
though a man's hand easily might dam its flow.

Racing past the first abandoned farmhouse,
bounding on beyond the village where the road starts,
gathering recruits, the stream requires a bridge and has a name.
It's on the map. Its cuts and curves are deeper
and its pace more dignified. It puts on weight.
The towns it passes are its progeny.
The squared-off, fertile fields to right and left
owe everything to this broad beam of water,
thing of use, this quiet and obliging beast of burden.
Men's hands, time and time again, have dammed its flow.
Its economic virtues overtake its lyrical.

In some part of its thwarted, interfered-with brain,
the creature has a memory, a long way back,
of when it roared, and playfully destroyed,
of when, at whim, it granted or withheld,
when men bowed down and prayed
and sacrificed that which they least could spare
in hope to earn the favour of a god.

The light of reason since has overtaken faith.
Its final service rendered, unresistingly
the animal gives up its great and broken heart
into that greater element
which no idea, no ingenuity has overtaken, yet.

# Chorus of the Guardian Cats of Montmartre Cemetery

*For Keith Fulton and Lou Pepe*

'Visitor with guide and camera, welcome to this solemn place.
Do not think of us as feral as you snap our feline grace.
We fulfil a sacred duty, guarding those who in their day
laid at France's feet their genius, and now offer her their clay.
Politicians, writers, painters, dancers, physicists here lie
high above the roofs of Paris, staring blindly at the sky.

You who come to render homage to these close-assembled greats,
(*Plan du Cimetière* to aid you), reading out their names and dates,
have no inkling of a power you would envy if you knew:
we are quadruped clairvoyants; we can see their spirits too.

★

A to Z, Ampère to Zola, Berlioz to Offenbach,
Degas, Heine, Fratellini flaunt their talents after dark.

Adolphe Sax, the late lamented, blows the horn that he invented.
Georges Feydeau, doyen of laughter, entertains the crowd hereafter.
Glimpsed beneath the evening star, *La Dame aux Camélias*.
Truffaut, as the light grows dim, re-releases *Jules et Jim*.
When the constellations peep, we observe Nijinsky's leap.
*Tristesse* born of lost caresses Dalida in song expresses.

Residents of every section of this municipal ground,
in collective resurrection fabled shades abound.
Stripped of all but heart and soul, they play their parts; and we patrol.

★

Hark! The closing bell is ringing. Make your way back to the gate.
Don't regret your forced departure. Paris's delights await.
Death is long. Here we've been keeping watch since 1825.
As you head off to the *Métro*, aren't you glad you're still alive?'

# Near Olmi-Cappella

In Corsica, the sun is strong
at midday in the last days of October:
old man determined to be young.

We sit all afternoon, the only customers,
outside the mountain restaurant.
Around us chestnut leaves drop, one by one.

The long meal closes. Coffee chills quickly
now a hill obscures the sun;
but the *signora* brings the *grappa* bottle on,

entrapped in solid ice, and in the ice
the flowers and fruits of spring and summer
reignite the seasons gone.

# Prepare for Landing

The plane banks, straightens, banks. The captain's voice:
'...a lovely day in Cape Town. On your right
is Table Mountain, and below us here
a view of Robben Island in the bay.
We have enjoyed your company, and bid
you all a proud South African farewell.'

How many years did planes bank, straighten, bank
and pass the dreadful place with nothing said?
'...a lovely day in Cape Town. On your right
is Table Mountain, and below us here
a view of Robben Island in the bay.
You can just glimpse our future president,
whom one day we shall always have admired.
We've done our best to break him and his kind.
He's at his morning exercise down there,
surviving, hoping, husbanding his strength.'

The man beside me, flying home, promotes
the island's 'fascinating history'.
He has been kind enough to share, all night,
his knowledge of the country: what to see,
which districts to avoid, what wines to try.
In desperation I was forced to write
and, when he asked me what it was, feign sleep.

Forgive, forget?
Oppressors grant themselves amnesia
by sole permission of the blessed fact
that the oppressed forgive.

# My Proper Life

Economy for twelve hours overnight
means total loss of feeling in the legs.
Tray tables back, seats up, good children all,
we fill in customs declaration forms,
my biro prodding anaesthetic knees.
I reach 'Profession'. Hmm. What am I, now
I don't go to the office any more?
I hesitate and then put 'Writer'. There.
I hope I'm not required to furnish proof.
'A list of publications, sir, perhaps?
A volume in your bag? No? I'm afraid…'

I get in with no trouble, and I've made
a kind of declaration to myself.
'I've just retired, and nothing's stopping me
from doing what I always said I would:
write poetry. And face the awful fact
that I might fail, might be embarrassing,
might make my friends seek kindly things to say
about the latest package in the post
I "hoped they might enjoy". So take the risk,
embarrass if you have to, what the hell.'

The legs are back in gear. The ears have popped
and all is ultra-clear and strange to sense:
the nosing rental car, bright light, warm wind,
November in the southern hemisphere.
Good child turned truant in my middle age,
I see that I've been looking out for signs,
for slip-roads to my proper life, for years.

# Two Epithalamia, Offering Similar Advice

**For David and Lindsay**

*Married at Rhydycroesau, 23 July 1994*

Round here is where the Saxon tangled with the Celt,
where tribal struggles and the lust for land
left scars, walls, dykes and ditches: markers and warnings
saying in either language, 'Here I stand.'

Today at Rhydycroesau, 'crossroads at the stream',
two ramblers come to wed. Both from the borders,
I know they like to walk the quiet Marches once patrolled
by sentries with a dangerous idea: the nation.
Poets, then as now, have special licence on occasion,
so here's my wedding gift of irresponsible advice.

Two persons are two countries, but let the boundary
be not too clearly marked. And live beyond your income (mostly).
Journey without maps – those of the heart are out of date
as soon as printed. Both when God's sun shines brightly
for you on the border hills, and facing time's adversity,
keep in each other's shadow, and be free.

## For Alix and Ben

*Married in Perth, Western Australia, 19 February 2016*

Poets have performed at weddings
since the ancient Greeks.
But it's still a risky moment
when the poet speaks.
Some too solemn; some too silly;
some whose rhyming creaks.

Thank you, Ben and Alix, that you
let this foreign poet in.
Will you take two words of counsel
from a licensed larrikin?
One is sober; one is silly;
with the sober I'll begin.

In the art of long-term loving
both must say their word.
It takes two for conversation;
neither is preferred.
Be yourselves; but let the line where
self and other meet be blurred.

That's the sober thought; and here's the
irresponsible advice:
Live beyond your income (mostly);
life is more than price.
Let your laughter be the coin you
never sacrifice.

I have done; so, with these others,
playing our supporting parts
to the leads you take as you
enact the union of your hearts,
I say: may your life, now joined,
transcend the joy in which it starts!

# Paul, I should like...

*To Paul Ashton*

Paul, I should like, one June, to fly with you once more
from Zurich to Lugano in that little jet
just when the morning sun has gained and overshot
the valley's eastern brim, so that our silhouette,
chasing the torrent, bounding over fields of light,
is fugitive as thought along its vivid floor.
A giant's thumb and finger gave the impetus
we'll feel inside this lemon pip's straight streak due south.
Great naked brutes of mountain heads will force our path
below, between them, frowning on our trespass.

And Elise will serve us champagne and cheese straws –
elevenses, or pre-*apéritifs* –
and we will smile in grateful disbelief
that such a moment, here again, is ours.

# 5

# New Style

Pope after pope has been aware that something must be done.
An ancient problem, worsening each year: the calendar
is straying from the sun. The vernal feast of Easter drifts
by tiny steps away from spring, towards the days of heat.

Pope Gregory is in his study with astronomers.
Their chief is Clavius the Jesuit, whose voice escapes
his lifetime's training in restraint. 'The remedy is here,
Your Holiness,' (he drums a paper) 'by God's help, at last.'

Pope Gregory's left hand shifts slightly. He is listening.

'Cut ten days from 1582,' says Clavius.
'Observe the saints' days lost the day before or after. Then,
in three of every four years which conclude the centuries
to come, omit the leap year. But retain the extra day
in 1600, and the year 2000, and so on.
The leap year (brainchild of an older Roman!) was indeed
a fine invention in its time, though not quite fine enough.'
He pauses for effect. 'Thus will the calendar remain
obedient to the sun for longer than three thousand years.'

Pope Gregory is satisfied. 'Prepare a Bull,' he says,
'and show me when it's written. Thank you, Christoph, gentlemen.'

The Bull is posted on the internet. I'm reading it
on leap year day 2000. It contains this very date,
the day that I am living in, foreseen, committed to:
an act of faith in reason... History unmakes itself,
the known reverts to the unknowable, and Clavius
is pointing out to Gregory a detail in the text.

'Your Holiness, the Day of Wrath may intervene before the date here written. In that case, Almighty God will see we have not sought to hasten His return before His will.'

The Pope is thinking that the wisdom of astronomers (and Jesuits) has not always been welcome to the Church, but says aloud, 'We wish it to be printed. Bring our seal.'

## Fabbro contro Falso

In Italy, in Dante's time, the lawyers' clerks
filled up the spaces at the ends of judgments, deeds and wills
with sonnets or with chunks of longer literary works
to thwart the later introduction of fake codicils:
professional scribes' forgeries appended
to parry or pervert the force intended
by careful phrasing in the body of the text.

And Dante's verses were employed as padding
against the practice of malicious adding.

Imagine it: a wealthy litigant has vexed
the patience of the court, and lost his case. In seething rage
he's flicking through the document confirming his defeat.
He finds ten tercets from *Inferno* on the final page.
He scans the visions of a cosmic dreamer,
the strange new numbers of the *terza rima,*
and sucks his teeth, and thinks of other ways to cheat.

# Too Much History

First there were only voices, and the use of memory.
Then paintings on cave walls.  Later,
when cities grew by rivers, and the merchants needed
something more permanent than simple trust,
pictures in miniature were proofs of contract.
So history began in the making of marks,
the blunt reed impressing the raw clay;
deliberation in the rows and columns of dark shapes
staining the pale ground of a scroll, a codex, book;
the chisel on the stele lauding the mighty.

Printing loosened, not the scribe's grip on the pen,
but the scribe's master's grip on his domain.
Yet for centuries more, the living,
looking back towards the country of the dead,
had meagre clues only as to its inhabitants:
writings, images, monuments.

                              Now, in a blink of time,
we have the means to tell all to the future.
Five hundred years from now, historians
and citizens in search of entertainment
will replay our every move – our working, sporting, mating,
killing one another – perfectly in focus, to the life,
our accents visiting their ears like ancient music.

There will be too much history for those remote spectators.
Glutted with information, they will turn away
from their exquisite screens, to seek relief
in that day's small events and unobserved routines.

# Legacy

What if, one day no different from the others
which in their trillions have come to pass
and passed away since energy's first flare,
since the Creation, Introit of the Universe,
Big Bang, whichever myth you find consoles
the brain hurt by considering such distances;
what if, like morning mist in warming air,
we humans were one day to disappear?

I mean just us, the planet's alpha males.
All other life remains. The species which stood up now falls
in some unique pandemic, or takes off into the sky –
a comprehensive Rapture which forgives us all.
The place we tended, forced and plundered echoes still
to calls of birds and beasts. Goldcrest and whale,
the rarest rhino and the common fly,
by us unhindered and unhunted, multiply.

Crops ripen till they rot where they were planted.
Blackened acres, bent before the wind,
are choked and toppled as the wilderness invades.
The grains – the careful work of our improving hand –
return directly to the glutted ground
where year by year they take their failing stand
against the vigour of uncultivated seeds.
Bramble and fern infringe the country roads.

Our settlements are silent, monochrome in dust,
their signs and images obscured, the meaning lost.
The tattered flags have nothing more to say.
Patiently, sunlight and rain, heat wave and frost
dismantle every structure we have built and leased
and grant their freehold to the dispossessed:
to creatures, plants and mould. A thousand years' decay
matters not much, is but the twinkling of an eye

except for this: the brews we now distil
to vaunt our mastery of nature spill
and burn into the world we've left. An age-long harm
is done, unless some microbe, finding to its taste
the morsels of our stubbornest perverted waste
can make a supper of it, which may be the last
meal taken in the earth's allotted time
until the sun consumes it and annihilates our crime.

# The Spider on my Copy of *The Origin of Species*

I swat the little creature with an idle hand.
It's hard enough, God knows (He does?), to understand
the patient man's great temple-shaking argument –
its beauteous intricacies equivalent
to those he found in barnacles or in sweet peas,
in growth of coral reefs, the work of worker bees –
without distractions to my barely coping brain.
Where was I? Concentrate. But here it is again!
I've read one paragraph, on pigeons; in that time,
by downward abseil and retracing upward climb,
it's back where first it suffered the mysterious blow,
its travelling as rapid as my reading's slow,
and goes about its lawful business, unafraid.
Well, let it be, and serve as living visual aid.
Spin out your steel, my murderer; ensnare your prey.
This book's an iron Bible you and I obey.

# The Rescuing of Starfish

*After 'The Star Thrower' by Loren Eiseley*

A little girl was running up and down the beach.
Her task: the rescuing of starfish, two at a time,
from hundreds stranded where the tide had left them.
Her journeys lengthened as the minutes passed.

Taking his daily walk along the hard wet sand,
a man stopped to admire her energy and work.
'If I don't do this, they will die,' she told him, breathless.
He smiled, but said, 'Look at them; there are hundreds.
How can you make a difference?'

Pausing just long enough
to wave the two she held in front of her, she said,
'I'll make a difference to these two.' Off she ran.

# Clouds

Constantly inconstant, merely water in air,
obedient to wind, they drift or stall or race;
obedient to temperature, from hour to hour
their passing presences disperse to empty space.

We try familiar comparisons; we say
they're formed of cotton wool, or curdled cream, or lace.
We liken them to animals or continents.
We spy in them a sailing ship, a giant's face.

We seekers of resemblances are like the clouds.
The force that drives the living planet drives us on.
We move, we change; we briefly catch the watcher's eye.
Unique we are, and insubstantial, and soon gone.

# Liberation

She's come back for her stuff, and for her children's stuff.
It's dangerous to be here, so she moves at speed
around the house she hasn't entered for a week,
since they escaped. *He* might come back. He might have tired
of seeking consolation in the local bars,
of getting men on stools, with nothing else to do,
to see his point of view. On each trip to the car
with bedding, clothes and toys, she checks the empty road.

She's hunting in the living room for photographs
of her the child, at home with mum and dad and cats,
of her the teenage star of school productions, her
on holiday near Pisa, by the sea, with mates
and boys, the year before she met him. Here they are
and there she is, or was. She liberates a few.
A sack is slumped against the television set.
She looks. 'Wank videos,' she mutters, and she turns

and there he is. A silence. And her hand goes straight
up to her throat to feel the place, still tender, where
he touched her last. 'Don't think you frighten me,' she says
and walks straight by him to the car. He makes no move.
She drives away, and suddenly a rush of joy
invades her, gaining speed between the winter fields,
though it has been so long since she has tasted it
that now she tastes it, it is hard to recognise.

# Leda Ponders Yeats's Sonnet

My *thighs* were *loosening*, in his account;
as if, after some struggle, I began
to overcome my terror of the swan
and please it in the role of willing mount.

My cunt was dry. The chafing made me bleed.
There was no *feathered glory*, no consent.
Its penis was its blood's blunt instrument
and blood was all that issued from the deed.

The poet asks if I, the raped, *put on*
the *knowledge with* the *power* of the beast
while it was in me. Did I get the taste
for knowing what the creature had foreknown?

Had ever screams been strangled in his throat,
he would have had his answer as he wrote.

# The Searchers

Cannibal seeks meal for special friendship.
Pensioner wants doll to be his wife.
Friendly girl needs escort for Barbados.
Widow longs to make new start in life.

Widower, who lost his wife to cancer,
writes to say he truly understands.
Escort is already in Barbados;
chalet on the beach, time on his hands.
Doll asks gentleman to make her British;
she will send her photo for keepsake.
Meal would like to meet before committing;
cooking's such a major step to take.

Cannibal agrees to meet – in secret;
eating meal's a risky thing to do.
Pensioner is thrilled by lovely photo;
maybe he can make doll's wish come true.
Friendly girl, who has a better offer,
won't be in Barbados after all.
Widow thanks the writer for his kindness;
leaves her number, should he care to call.

Widower is plucking up his courage;
turns from the computer to the phone.
Escort in Barbados leaves the café,
feeling unattractive and alone.
Doll needs money, sponsor for her visa
and mister please when is the wedding date?
Meal has finger on apartment buzzer;
still in time to choose another fate.

Dreamland achieved! Vast, secret playground
where perfect strangers huddle and conspire
and millions of tense, two-fingered typists
edge towards enactments of desire.

# At a Banking Crisis

The houses of usury go to the wall.
The higher the fliers, the broader the sky
and gravity's merely a force to defy.
How could they have known that their engines would stall?

The pilots are limping away from the crash.
The crimes they committed they stoutly deny
(the bolder the gambler, the bigger the lie);
and could we oblige with the loan of some cash?

Magnificent men in their money machines!
We feel in our pockets and fish out some change.
The ways of the Lord (that is Mammon) are strange;
and we're all of us dead in the long run, said Keynes.

# The Prisoner

I try to make my mind a whitewashed wall
but memory defaces its expanse.
Each human sound which penetrates the cell
recalls the roar my voice excited once.

I spoke, and hopeless people's hopes were stirred.
In province after province, speech by speech,
I earned the acclamation of the crowd.

None could deny I had the leader's touch;
to get the leadership was easy. Then
the hard task came: to form a single force
where local law and loyalty had been.

Our kindred had a prior claim on us.
Despite the government's barbarity
our fellowship in arms was incomplete.
Why is the use of fear the only way?
I made examples, which I now regret.

Throughout the shifting motives of the time,
I pleaded with the soldiers to keep sight
of our idea. I told myself its flame
burned still in each day's orders.

                    I found out
that nearest friends are false, and here I am.
I try to keep my mind a private room
but politics come picking at its lock.
So far from battle drifts the battle smoke.

# Epiphany 2006

The year is only nearly new.
The house is plain once more.
My life so free and prosperous:
I thank you, luck of draw.

Just as we tire of feasting
here comes another feast.
Messiah has been recognised
by Gentiles from the East.

To set beside the tributes
my holy book records
my only contribution is
these inexpensive words:

'In Israel, would-be Palestine,
Iraq, Afghanistan,
the evidence is scanty
of the brotherhood of man.

When Christians, Muslims, Jews exchange
their gifts of hate and fear
and not a token truce detains
destruction's working year;

when Herod and the priests compete
to bring the greater grief
by lust for land and power,
by perversion of belief;

when *love your neighbour as yourself*'s
a thought best left unsaid;
when mothers only have their tears
to wet their baby's head;

this much we see, by reason's light,
and not a guiding star's:
the madness in religion
and the wickedness in wars.'

The caravan has packed and gone,
gone home another way.
For now, the wise men see no point
in lengthening their stay.

# Wedding Party

The village wedding guests will not forget
their children charred and broken where they lie.
We haven't won the war on terror yet.

Terrors by night, a gunship and a jet
have handed down destruction from on high.
Bewailing witnesses will not forget.

The pilots thought their planes were under threat
from rifles fired for joy into the sky.
These tribal customs haven't died out yet.

A military statement of regret
will not bring back the apples of their eye
to folk who trust in God not to forget.

The act has made of boys whose cheeks were wet
God's warriors whose holy rage is dry.
We haven't cured this twisted thinking yet.

Beheadings posted on the internet?
What savages these people are, we cry.
The warriors are sworn not to forget.
We'll stay the course. The job's not finished yet.

# The Zealots

Sure of their rightness, and their righteousness, they kill.
To them, the blood's well spent. Its creeping tide sustains
a purity of energy within their brains,
the undistracted operation of their will.

We are their enemy, the doubters, we who see
survival in the strength of hybrid, motley things;
the rage from which their readiness to murder springs
is fuelled by contempt for our uncertainty.

Reluctant we may be, yet we must take a stand
against their zeal, must find a single voice to say
that various is what we are, how we shall stay,
that certainty in their terms desolates a land.

Confessors of all sorts have stirred the mob before.
Our unity in difference, our faith in thought,
the patient force of reason: only these may thwart
the soldiers of the inquisition at the door.

# A Hope Denied

It started when Mohamed set himself alight:
a blaze of rage, ignited by a single spark.
That hopeful flame now gutters, and the scene is almost dark
and heroes who, these thirty months, have dared to claim the right

to certain simple freedoms, which they briefly won,
are robbed of them by two kinds of barbarian:
the one loud-hails perversions of the word of God to man;
the other needs no mouthpiece but the yawning of a gun.

# Drummer

The boy enlisted, as he thought,
to serve his country's good;
but violence that we export
returns to source in blood.

Stock tributes to his sacrifice
we piously repeat.
It's drummer boys who pay the price
for drums their elders beat.

# Out of City

Where is it leading, this unlovely highway,
potholed main drag, bruised and beaten track?

*Across the river, to the city limits.*
*Onward to the mountains or the sea.*

Where are they going, these encumbered travellers,
saying little, never looking back?

*As if they knew. They only know the city*
*which was theirs is not theirs. So they flee.*

What might they hope for at their destination?
*Simple safety and a queue for bread.*

Will acts of special kindness in this crisis
ease the hardship of the road ahead?

*Unfortunately not. The human virtues*
*falter in conditions of distress.*

What is the meaning of this mass displacement?
*Search for it in human wickedness.*

# Inauguration Day: January 2017

*After Robert Lowell*

A braggart, whom we thought absurd,
a master of the wounding word,
combining vanity with hate
is now Commander of the State.

Democracy's a savaged plant.
The credulous, the ignorant,
who trust in God, forgive his sins.
America's worst angel wins.

The plant is bleeding from its stump
as the Republic summons Trump.
Doyen of feral billionaires,
he lifts the hand that grabs, and swears.

Cold tears are leaking from the sky.
How sure success is when you lie!

# Pleasure's Bargain

*After Donne's 'To his Mistress Going to Bed'*

True, madam, true: only a fool would try
to imitate John Donne in poetry.
And I'm that fool. The lapse of centuries
has not reduced the power of striptease
to hold a lady's visitor in thrall.
Too slowly, yet too fast, your garments fall;
you toy with my desires, you draw my eyes
'above, below'; my rising fancy tries
to peep through those adornments which remain
and, in my mock frustration, I complain
I don't know if my libido's compelled
the more by what's displayed or what withheld.

The sequence of disrobing Donne sets down
– the girdle first, the breast-plate, busk, the gown,
the coronet, hose, shoes – differs not much
from what my mistress knows I like to watch.
For 'busk' read 'basque'; for 'breast-plate', 'bra'; I know
that girdles now come later in the show.
The gowns you wear (petite) enlarge my lust
and, what is more, they won't drag in the dust.
I am of Cromwell's party, don't forget;
your queenly beauty needs no coronet.
Some difference there is, your lover thinks,
between the great and minor poets' kinks.
For me, no carnal pleasure can compare
with that supplied by flimsy underwear.
Donne reaches climax through full nudity:

'Off,' 'Off,' 'Make shift to shift that shift,' cries he.
Your latter-day but no less ardent John
prefers you with your shoes and stockings on.

'America! my new-found-land', 'My Mine':
he, libertine (but soon-to-be divine),
saw sex in terms of England v. the Rest;
he plundered her as soon as she undressed.
We know where such equivalences led:
the rape of nations, and the millions dead;
the victor's excess of testosterone –
'I come, I see, I ravish, and I own.'
(Or should 'I come', instead of first, come third?)
Madam, you ravish me by deed and word.

Forgive that sudden change of tone of voice;
sometimes a poem's not a poet's choice.
Now you are nearly naked, but not quite,
undress your man, and take your own delight.
Don't be 'My Mine', be mine; this bargain's made
between two friendly countries, as fair trade.
These couplets ended, you and I are free
to couple for our pleasure, equally.

# Good Friday, 2013. Driving Westward

*After Donne's 'Good-Friday, 1613. Riding Westward'*

Lately the lover, shortly to be priest,
although 'my Soules forme bends toward the East',
his horse's head faced firmly to the west.
'Pleasure or businesse' called him, he confessed,
despite the new 'devotion' he had learned
to One who suffered while his back was turned.

And is 'mans Soule', as he proposed, 'a Spheare',
subject to sudden lurches of career
as other spheres exert their influence,
distracting reason by the lure of sense?
(His light of reason was the fire of faith,
sparked by 'a Sunne' who, setting, banished death.)
I would say yes; and we part company
only in this: reason and sense for me
act on the soul merely within the skull.
I know no other, outer Agent's pull.

Donne knew an Other; in his memory
he sees Christ in His bloody agony,
'Made durt of dust', that sinners might be clean.
His mind relives the drama of the scene:
darkness at noon, the cracking of the rocks.
He argues for his faith by paradox.
The hands that 'tune all spheares', so wide their 'span',
though 'peirc'd with... holes', still play upon this man;

in him, the Master of the universe
is dextrous in resolving Adam's curse.
On this 'good' Friday, best and worst of days,
with reins and whip in hand the rider prays
the All-in-All who made Himself as nought,
consenting to be mocked and flayed for sport,
to scourge his back to make his sickness whole.
Christ's gravity is hauling in his soul.

He cantered and I drive through Warwickshire
this evening in the hesitating year,
both heading into Wales's baffled spring.
What comfort can a real sunset bring
now God is dead and shut up in the tomb
and it is hard to say, 'Thy kingdom come,'
even for one who, to his soul, believed?
And yet — his final paradox achieved —
if 'Soules' be 'Spheares' and rolling westward, we
will come at last to that from which we flee.

# As John Donne Tells Us...

'No man is an island'; and no man wrote a truer word.
The human continent's a reciprocity of need.
In his conceit we're Europe: manor, clod or promontory.
Yet each piece of the continent, each man's 'part of the main',
is governed by a monarch who divides and rules the brain,
as reason, dreams and appetites contest supremacy.
No one of these prevails, nor yields. No truce will be agreed
until the bell which 'tolls for thee', and you hear not, is heard.

# Her Night Thoughts

The love he rarely brings me,
differently and long,
I keep here in a chamber
whose lock and key are strong.
No other song
rhymes with the songs he sings me.

The moments of our meeting
are brief and widely spaced;
our slow anticipation
has never been misplaced.
Lovely each taste
of joining and completing.

Tonight, when sleep deserts me
and solo thoughts are free,
I re-enact the pleasures
we take in company.
The more I see,
the more the absence hurts me.

How may I rediscover
my easiness of mind?
I turn the key and open
the chamber I designed;
wherein I find
a rhyme left by my lover.

The music of the verses,
their movement and their sway,
perform this token service:
to shorten the delay
until the day
for which my mind rehearses.

# 6

# Pupil to Teacher

*To Peter Hetherington, my English teacher 1965–1969*

The pupil, like the child, assumes this privilege:
to take for granted what is given. Even so,
we knew by instinct that your teacher's gift was rare:
the mix of tenderness and ardour for the books
you showed us into; your glad welcome for the valid thought
the learning brain sometimes put forth, spotted unerringly
and sorted from the mawkish airs
and trying-on of other people's scholarship
of teenage intellectuals; the boldness of your judgments –
telling us, in 1966,
that *Godot* is as great a play as *Lear* –
it took my breath away and gave it back.
Even your rages – annual, in March,
when play rehearsals hit a crisis – cried out loud
that going through the motions was the least of it,
that we could be in step, if only we'd step up,
with language which would tip-toe out of bounds
and leave us wiser than our masters…

                      Nearly 40 years have passed
and I've come back to thank you. Why so long?
Not sloth, forgetfulness or busyness; I needed all that time
to make a little heap of verses good enough
to say to you that greatness in a teacher
has its consequences; master, these are one.

# At His Quitting Time

*In honour of Seamus Heaney*

To me, your novice, you were more than master. You were mage.
Your books were talismans I reached for countless times, in hope
to hear the magic word which would unlock me, spring me,
    do the trick.
Foolish apprentice, seeking short cuts! I had no such luck.
Between your lines a truer, slower voice spoke up, and still speaks up,
its Derry accent urging, 'Take the plunge.
Practise the art. Go on now. You can do it.'

               When you left
it was late August, and your blackberries were ripening.
Beside your house of death, next to the low clay roof, what can I leave
as grave gift but the debt – unpayable – you must forgive?
This afternoon, as summer lingers, I'm out plundering
the hedges, as you did. I'm burdened and bereft.

Poems, berries, season's fullness… I can't help trying
the comparison, until I see its flaw.
Your childhood's hoarded treasures rotted and went sour.
Your lifetime's hoard of words retains the staying power to bless
and strengthen us who stay and grieve. But will not now increase.
For that loss, as you did, I feel like crying.

# In Memoriam Stephen John Eyers, 1943–2016

To say it briefly, my best friend has died.
And I have no defence, no refuge from the fact,
except that, this side of the great divide,
my portion of our love is still intact.

Socialist in politics and humanist in faith,
he 'dwelt in possibility', so that his mind
perceived in history's best moments pointers,
not anomalies, despite their brevity:
Winstanley's Commonwealth, the Communards,
the days of Barcelona '36 or Britain '45
were bold illuminations of the good society
on which he fixed his stubborn, hopeful eye.

We were two Hampshire boys, lapsed Protestants,
both gaily on the run from all that nonsense:
sin, guilt, sexual shame – the whole bang-shoot of lies.
A true adherent of 'the mystery of things',
he saw the sacramental in the ordinary.
He lived as if our purpose here is joy.

He was a teacher for whom *teach* and *learn* are synonyms.

The passing months do nothing but lay bare my loss
and Christmas only plays again the scenes I miss:
our greeting on the phone, a thousand times, if once –
my 'Stevie!', his 'Hello, dear boy!' – call and response;
David and Jonathan, our frank, unshaven hug.
He lies in earth in Surrey, where the Diggers dug.

# The Poet's Prayer

Poetry is just consonants and vowels.
Mostly it's like crapping when you don't want to.
Muse, move in a mysterious way within my bowels.

Poetry is just thoughts tricked out in lines.
It's like watching for shooting stars in August.
Lord, let me not be blinking when one shines.

Poetry is just management of stress.
On wonderful days it's like taking dictation.
God, grant me such days more often, and the others less.